The Expulsion of the Other

Byung-Chul Han

The Expulsion of the Other

Society, Perception and
Communication Today

Translated by Wieland Hoban

polity

First published in German as *Die Austreibung des Anderen* © S. Fischer Verlag GmbH, Frankfurt am Main, 2016

This English edition © Polity Press, 2018

Polity Press
65 Bridge Street
Cambridge CB2 1UR, UK

Polity Press
101 Station Landing
Suite 300
Medford, MA 02155, USA

ISBN-13: 978-1-5095-2305-4
ISBN-13: 978-1-5095-2306-1 (pb)

A catalogue record for this book is available from the British Library.

Library of Congress Cataloging-in-Publication Data

Names: Han, Byung-Chul, author.
Title: The expulsion of the other : society, perception and communication today / Byung-Chul Han.
Description: English edition. | Cambridge, UK : Medford, MA, USA : Polity Press, [2018] | Includes bibliographical references and index.
Identifiers: LCCN 2017033814 (print) | LCCN 2017036604 (ebook) | ISBN 9781509523092 (Epub) | ISBN 9781509523054 (hardback) | ISBN 9781509523061 (pbk.)
Subjects: LCSH: Fear--Social aspects. | Other (Philosophy)
Classification: LCC HM1071 (ebook) | LCC HM1071 .H36 2018 (print) | DDC
302/.17--dc23
LC record available at https://lccn.loc.gov/2017033814

Typeset in 11.5 on 15 pt Janson Text by
Servis Filmsetting Limited, Stockport, Cheshire
Printed and bound in Great Britain by CPI Group (UK) Ltd, Croydon

For further information on Polity, visit our website:
politybooks.com

CONTENTS

1

The Terror of the Same

The time in which there was such a thing as the *Other* is over. The Other as a secret, the Other as a temptation, the Other as eros, the Other as desire, the Other as hell and the Other as pain disappear. The negativity of the Other now gives way to the positivity of the Same. The proliferation of the Same constitutes the pathological changes that afflict the social body. It is made sick not by denial and prohibition, but by over-communication and over-consumption; not by suppression and negation, but by permissiveness and affirmation. The pathological sign of our times is not repression but depression. Destructive pressure comes not from the Other but from within.

Depression as internal pressure develops auto-aggressive traits. The depressive performance subject[1] is as it were beaten down or suffocated by the self. Not only the violence of the Other is destructive; the expulsion of the Other sets in motion an entirely different process of destruction, namely that of *self-destruction*. In general, the dialectic of violence applies: *a system that rejects the negativity of the Other develops self-destructive traits.*

The violence of the Same is invisible because of its positivity. The proliferation of the Same presents itself as growth. At a certain point, however, production is no longer productive but destructive, information is no longer informative but deformative, and communication is no longer communicative but merely cumulative.

Today, perception itself takes the form of 'binge-watching'. This refers to the consumption of videos and films without any temporal restrictions. The consumers are continuously offered those films and series that match their taste, and therefore *please* them. Like consumer livestock, they are fattened with ever-new sameness. Binge-watching can be generalized as *the* contemporary mode of perception. The proliferation of the Same resembles not a carcinoma but a coma, and does not meet with any immunological defences. One goggles oneself into unconsciousness.

The cause of an infection is the negativity of the Other, who infiltrates the Same and leads to the formation of antibodies. The infarction, on the other hand, comes from an excess of the Same, from the obesity of the system. It is not infectious but adipose. Fat creates no antibodies. No immunological defence can prevent the proliferation of the Same..

The negativity of the *Other* provides form and measure for the *Selfsame*; without it, the *Same* proliferates.[2] The Selfsame is not identical to the Same; it always appears in tandem with the Other. The Same, by contrast, lacks

2

a dialectical counterpart that can limit and form it, and thus proliferates into a formless mass. The Selfsame has a form, an inner collectedness, an inwardness that is due to its *difference from the Other*. The Same, however, is formless. As it lacks dialectical tension, it leads to an indifferent collection, a sprawling mass of indistinguishability.

We can only say 'the selfsame' if we think difference. It is in the carrying out and settling of differences that the gathering nature of the selfsame comes to light. The selfsame banishes all zeal always to level what is different into the same. The selfsame gathers what is distinct into an original being-at-one. The same, on the contrary, disperses them into the dull unity of mere uniformity.[3]

The terror of the Same affects all areas of life today. One travels everywhere, yet does not *experience* anything. One catches sight of everything, yet reaches no *insight*. One accumulates information and data, yet does not attain *knowledge*. One lusts after adventures and stimulation, but always remains *the same*. One accumulates online 'friends' and 'followers', yet never encounters another person. Social media constitutes an absolute zero grade of the social.

Total interconnection and total communication by digital means does not facilitate encounters with Others. Rather, it serves to pass over those who are unfamiliar and other, and instead find those who are the same or like-minded, ensuring that our horizon of experience becomes ever narrower. It draws us into an endless ego loop, ultimately leading to an 'autopropaganda, indoctrinating us with our own ideas'.[4]

3

The negativity of the Other and of transformation is what constitutes experience in an emphatic sense. To have an experience of something means 'that this something befalls us, strikes us, comes over us, overwhelms and transforms us'.⁵ Its essence is *pain*. The same, however, is not painful. Today, pain gives way to an online 'like', which continues the Same.

Information is simply available. Knowledge in an emphatic sense, however, is a long and slow process. It displays an entirely different temporality. It *matures*. *Maturation* is a temporality that we are increasingly losing today. It is not compatible with today's politics of time, which fragments time and eliminates temporally stable structures in order to increase efficiency and productivity.

Even the largest accumulation of information, Big Data, possesses very little knowledge. Big Data is used to find correlations. A correlation states: when A occurs, B often also occurs. It is not *known*, however, *why* this is so. Correlation is the most primitive form of knowledge, being not even capable of ascertaining the relationship between cause and effect. *It is so*. The question of why becomes irrelevant; thus nothing is *understood*. But knowledge is understanding. Hence Big Data renders thought superfluous. We surrender ourselves without concern to the it-is-so.

Thought has access to the entirely Other. It can interrupt the Same; therein lies its event character. Calculation, on the other hand, is an endless repetition of the Same; in contrast to thought, it cannot produce any new state. It is *blind to the event*. True thought, however, is eventful. The French word for 'digital' is *numérique*. The numerical makes everything countable and comparable. Thus it perpetuates the Same.

Insight[6] in an emphatic sense is also transformative. It produces a new state of consciousness. Its structure resembles that of a redemption, providing more than the solution to a problem. It puts those in need of redemption in an entirely different state of being.

In his text 'Love and Knowledge', Max Scheler points out that Augustine ascribes to plants 'in mysterious ways' a longing to be looked at by humans, 'as though what happens to plants through love-derived insight is a kind of analogue of [. . .] redemption'.[7] If a flower had a fullness of being within itself it would not feel a need to be looked at; hence it has a lack, a lack of being. The loving gaze, a 'love-derived insight', *redeems* it from the state of lack. It is thus an 'analogue of redemption'. *Insight is redemption.* It has a loving relation to its object as something *Other*. This is where it differs from mere cognizance or information, which entirely lacks the dimension of the Other.

Negativity inheres in the event, for it brings with it a new relationship with reality, a new world, a new understanding of what *is*. It suddenly places everything in an entirely different light. Heidegger's 'forgetfulness of being' means nothing other than this *event-blindness*. Heidegger would say that today's communication noise, the *digital flurry* of data and information, deafens us to the noiseless roar of the truth, to its *silent violence*: 'A roar: it is / truth itself / stepped among / mankind, / right into the / metaphor-flurry.'[8]

The beginnings of the digital revolution were dominated above all by utopian projects. Flusser, for example, elevated digital interconnection to the technology of altruism. Being-human then means being-connected to Others. Digital interconnection supposedly enables a

5

special experience of resonance. Everything resonates sympathetically:

> The net vibrates, it is a pathos, it is a resonance. That is the foundation of telematics, this sympathy and antipathy of proximity. I believe that telematics is a technology of altruism, a technology for the implementation of Judeo-Christianity. The basis of telematics is empathy. It eliminates humanism in favour of altruism. The mere fact that this is possible is already quite colossal.[9]

Today, the net changes into a special resonant space, an echo chamber purged of all otherness, all foreignness. True resonance presupposes the *proximity* of the Other. Today, the proximity of the Other gives way to the gaplessness of the Same. Global communication only permits equal Others or other equals.[10]

Distance is inscribed in closeness as its dialectical counterpart. The abolition of distance does not create more closeness, but rather destroys it. Instead of closeness, a complete gaplessness ensues. Closeness and distance are interwoven, kept together by a dialectical tension. This tension consists in the fact that things are given life precisely by their opposite, by that which is other than themselves. A mere positivity like gaplessness lacks this animating force. Closeness and distance dialectically mediate each other like the Selfsame and the Other. Thus, neither gaplessness nor the Same are alive.

Digital gaplessness removes all varieties of proximity and distance. Everything is equally near and equally far: 'Trace and aura. The trace is appearance of a nearness, however far removed the thing that left it may be. The aura is appearance of a distance, however close the thing that calls it forth.'[11] The negativity of the Other, the foreign, the enigma, inheres in the aura. The digital society of transparency de-auratizes and de-mystifies the world. Over-closeness and over-exposure, as the general pictorial effect of porn, destroy any auratic distance, which also characterizes the erotic.

In porn, all bodies are alike. They also consist of equal body parts. Robbed of all language, the body is reduced to the sexual, which knows no difference apart from gender. The pornographic body is no longer a site, a 'sumptuous theatre', the 'fabulous surface of the inscription of dreams and divinities'.[12] It relates nothing. It does not seduce. Pornography carries out a complete de-narrativization and de-lingualization not only of the body, but of communication as such; therein lies its obscenity. It is impossible to *play* with the naked flesh. Play requires an *illusion*, an *untruth*. Naked, pornographic truth permits no play, no seduction. Sexuality as functional performance likewise drives out all forms of play; it becomes entirely mechanical. The neoliberal imperative of performance, sexiness and fitness ultimately reduces the body to a functional object that is to be optimized.

The proliferation of the Same is 'the full through which only the empty appears'.[13] The expulsion of the Other produces an *adipose emptiness of fullness*. What is obscene is the hypervisibility, hypercommunication, hyperproduction and hyperconsumption that lead to a rushing standstill of the Same. What is obscene is the 'perpetual engendering of the same by the same'.[14] Seduction, by contrast, is the power 'to tear the same away from the same',[15] to make it deviate from itself. The subject of seduction is the *Other*.

7

Its mode is *play* as the counter-mode to performance and production. Today, even play is transformed into a form of production; work is *gamified*.

Charlie Kaufman's stop-motion film *Anomalisa* mercilessly depicts today's hell of sameness; it could equally have been called *Longing for the Other* or *In Praise of Love*. In the hell of sameness, no *desire for the Other* is possible. The protagonist, Michael Stone, is a successful motivation trainer and author. His bestselling volume is entitled *How Can I Help You Help Them?*, a typical self-help guide for the neoliberal world. The book is universally acclaimed because it considerably increases productivity. Despite his success, he finds himself in a major existential crisis. He seems lonely, lost, bored, disillusioned and disoriented in a meaningless, monotonous, polished society of consumerism and performance. Its denizens all have the same face and speak in the same voice. The voice of the taxi driver, the waitress or the hotel manager is identical to that of his wife or his ex-girlfriend. The face of a child is no different from that of an adult. The world is peopled by clones, yet each paradoxically wants to be different from the others.

Michael goes to Cincinnati to give a lecture. At the hotel he hears a woman's voice that sounds entirely different. He knocks at the door of what he assumes to be her room; he finds her. To his surprise, she recognizes him. She has come to Cincinnati to hear his lecture. She has not only a different voice but also a different face; yet she finds herself ugly, as her face deviates from the optimized standard one. She is also chubby and has a facial scar that she tries to hide behind her hair. But Michael falls in love with her, with her different voice, with her otherness, with her anomaly. Intoxicated with love, he calls her Anomalisa. They spend the night together. In a nightmare, Michael is pursued by completely identical hotel staff who want to have sex with him; he wanders through a hell of sameness. At breakfast, he is alarmed to find that Lisa's voice is becoming increasingly like the standard voice. He returns home. The desert of sameness is everywhere. His family and friends welcome him, but he cannot tell them apart; they are all the same. Totally confused, he finds himself looking at an old Japanese sex doll that he bought for his son at a sex shop. Her mouth is wide open, ready to fellate.

In the final scene, Lisa affirms her love for Michael as if from another world, seemingly liberated from the spell of sameness, in which everyone is given back their own voice and their own face. Lisa tells him in passing that Anomalisa means 'sky goddess' in Japanese. Anomalisa is the epitome of the Other who saves us from the hell of sameness. She is *the Other as eros*.

In that hell of sameness, humans are nothing but remote-controlled puppets. It therefore makes sense that the film was indeed made with puppets, not real actors. The treacherous cracks in Michael's face make him sense that he is now only a puppet. In one scene, part of his face falls off; he holds the piece of his mouth, which automatically babbles something. He is shocked by the fact that he is a puppet. Büchner's statement that 'We are puppets, drawn with wire by unknown forces; nothing, nothing is ourselves!' could probably have served as the film's tagline.

9

2

The Violence of the Global and Terrorism

Globalization has an inherent violence that makes everything interchangeable, comparable and thus the same. Ultimately, this total equalization leads to a negation of meaning; meaning is something incomparable.[1] Yet money creates neither meaning nor identity. The violence of the global as the violence of the Same destroys the negativity of the Other, of the singular, of the incomparable, which impairs the circulation of information, communication and capital. It is precisely where the Same encounters the Same that this circulation reaches its highest velocity.

The violence of the global, which levels out everything into the same and establishes a hell of sameness, produces a destructive counterforce. Jean Baudrillard has already pointed out that the madness of globalization creates terrorists as madmen. This would mean that the prison camp at Guantánamo Bay corresponds to the asylums and prisons of that repressive disciplinary society which itself produces delinquents and psychopaths.

With terrorism, something has happened that points beyond the immediate intention of its actors to systemic fractures. It is not the religious itself that drives people to terrorism. Rather, it is the resistance of the singular to the violence of the global. A defence against terror that is directed at particular regions and groups of people is therefore a helpless substitute act. Invoking the enemy likewise conceals the true problem, which has a systemic cause. It is the terror of the global itself that produces terrorism.

The violence of the global sweeps away all singularities that do not submit to universal exchange. Terrorism is the terror of the singular against the terror of the global. Death, which eludes all exchange, is the epitome of the singular. In the shape of terrorism, it bursts brutally into the system where life is totalized as production and performance. Death is the end of production. The glorification of death by the terrorists and today's health hysteria, which attempts to prolong life as mere life at all costs, are mutually dependent. Al-Qaeda's motto draws attention to this systemic connection: 'You love life, we love death.'

Jean Baudrillard refers to the architectural particularity of the Twin Towers, which had already been the target of an Islamic terrorist attack in 1993. Whereas the high-rise buildings of the Rockefeller Center reflect the city and the sky in their glass and steel fronts, the Twin Towers have no connection to the outside, no connection to the Other. The two twin buildings, which resemble each other and

11

reflect each other, form a closed system. Thus the *Same* established itself in a total exclusion of the Other. The terrorist attack puts cracks in this global *system of sameness*. Today's reawakening nationalism, the New Right or the Identitarian movement, are likewise reflex reactions to the dominance of the global. It is no coincidence, therefore, that the followers of the New Right are not only xenophobic but also critical of capitalism. Both the national-romantic praise of borders and Islamist terrorism follow the same reactive schema in the face of the global. Neoliberalism produces massive injustice at the global level; exploitation and exclusion are constitutive of it. It sets up a 'banopticon' that identifies those who are hostile or unsuited to the system as undesirable and excludes them. The Panopticon serves to discipline, while the banopticon provides security. Neoliberalism even exacerbates social injustice within the zone of Western affluence; ultimately, it abolishes the social market economy. The originator of the term 'neoliberalism', Alexander Rüstow, had already noted that a society governed entirely by the laws of the neoliberal market would become inhumane and create social fractures. Accordingly, he points out that neoliberalism must be augmented by a 'politics of vitality' [*Vitalpolitik*] that brings about solidarity and community spirit. Without this politics of life as a corrective, neoliberalism results in insecure, fear-driven masses that can easily be co-opted by ethno-nationalistic forces. Here the fear of one's own future turns into xenophobia. Fear for oneself is manifested not only as hatred of strangers, but also as self-hatred. The society of fear and the society of hatred are mutually dependent.

Social insecurities, coupled with a lack of hope or perspectives, also provide fertile soil for terrorist forces. The neoliberal system virtually breeds these only seemingly opposed destructive elements. In reality, the Islamic terrorist and the ethno-nationalist are not enemies but siblings, for they share the same genealogy. Money is a poor bestower of identity. It can replace identity, however, for money gives its owner at least a feeling of security and calm. Someone who does not even have money, however, has nothing – neither identity nor security. Thus they are forced into the imaginary, for example the ethnic perspective, which quickly provides an identity. In so doing, they invent an *enemy* for themselves, such as Islam. Hence one builds up *immunities* via imaginary channels in order to arrive at a meaningful identity. *Fear for oneself* unconsciously fosters a longing for the enemy. The enemy, even in imaginary form, is a fast supplier of identity: 'The enemy is our own question as *Gestalt*. [. . .] For this reason, I must confront him in battle in order to arrive at my own standard, my own bounds, my own *Gestalt*.'[2] The imaginary compensates for what is lacking in reality. Terrorists likewise inhabit the imaginary. The global creates imaginary spaces that provoke actual violence.

The violence of the global simultaneously weakens the immune defence, which hinders the accelerated global circulation of information and capital. It is precisely in those places where the immune thresholds are very low that capital flows more quickly. Within the currently predominant order of the global, which totalizes the Same, there are only really *equal Others* or *other equals*.[3] *Fantasies for Others* do not awaken at the newly erected border

13

fences. They are speechless. In reality, immigrants and refugees are not *Others* either, not *strangers* that create the feeling of an actual threat, of real fear. That threat exists only in the imaginary realm; immigrants and refugees are seen more as a burden. As possible neighbours they are objects of resentment and envy, which, in contrast to dread, fear and disgust, are not genuine immunological reactions. The xenophobic masses may be against North Africans, but they go to their countries for package tours.

For Baudrillard, the violence of the global is carcinomatous. It spreads like 'cancerous cells' through 'endless proliferation, excrescence and metastasis'.[4] He uses an immunological model to explain the global: 'All the talk of immunity, antibodies, grafting and rejection should not surprise anyone.'[5] The violence of the global is 'a viral violence, that of networks and the virtual'.[6] Virtuality is viral. What is problematic is this immunological description of interconnection; immunities restrict the circulation of information and communication. A Facebook 'like' is not an immunological reaction. The violence of the global as the violence of positivity is *post-immunological*. Baudrillard overlooks this paradigm shift, which is constitutive of the digital, neoliberal order. Immunities are part of the earthly order. Jenny Holzer's injunction, 'Protect me from what I want,' precisely demonstrates the post-immunological quality of the violence of positivity.

'Infection', 'grafting', 'rejection' and 'antibodies' do not explain today's excess of over-communication and over-information. The excess of the Same can lead to vomiting, but this is different from a disgust towards the Other, the unfamiliar. Disgust is 'a state of alarm and

14

emergency, an acute crisis of self-assertion in the face of an unassimilable otherness'.[7] It is precisely the missing negativity of the Other that provokes such symptoms as bulimia, binge-watching or binge-eating. They are not viral; rather, they stem from the violence of positivity, which eludes any immune defence.

Neoliberalism is anything but the endpoint of the Enlightenment. It is not guided by reason. It is precisely its lunacy that produces destructive tensions which erupt in the form of terrorism and nationalism. The freedom which neoliberalism purports to be is an advertisement. Today, the global even appropriates universal values; thus freedom itself is exploited. People willingly exploit themselves under the illusion of realizing themselves. It is not the suppression of freedom, but rather its exploitation that maximizes productivity and efficiency. This is the perfidious logic that underlies neoliberalism.

In the face of the violence of the global, the concern must be to protect the universal from co-option by the global. It is therefore necessary to invent a universal order that also opens up to the singular. That singular, which irrupts violently into the system of the global, is not the Other who would permit a dialogue. The diabolical nature of terrorism lies in the impossibility of dialogue that characterizes it. The singular would only give up its diabolical nature in a reconciled state in which it remained the distant, different element in the midst of the closeness provided.[8]

Kant's 'perpetual peace' is nothing other than the state of reconciliation. It rests on *universal* values that reason provides for itself. According to Kant, peace is also forced by the 'spirit of trade, which cannot coexist with war, and which will, sooner or later, take hold of every people'.[9] But it is temporary, not perpetual. It is only the 'power of money' that forces peace for its own purposes. Global trade is a war by other means, however, as Goethe's *Faust* has already conveyed: 'What seaman does not take for granted / The undivided trinity / Of war and trade and piracy?'[10]

The violence of the global produces deaths and refugees in the same way as a true world war. The peace forced by the spirit of trade is not only temporary but also geographically restricted. The zone of affluence, or in fact the island of affluence as a banopticon, is surrounded by border fences, refugee camps and theatres of war. Kant presumably failed to recognize the diabolical, indeed reasonless nature of the spirit of trade. His judgement was lenient; he assumed it would bring about a 'long' peace. But this peace is a mere illusion. The spirit of trade's only remaining talent is calculation. It lacks all reason. Hence a system governed purely by the spirit of trade, the power of money, is itself reasonless.

Today's refugee crisis makes it especially clear that the European Union is no more than an economic trading union guided by self-interest. The EU as a European free-trade zone, a treaty community comprising governments and their nation-state interests, is not what Kant would consider a product of reason, a reason-based 'league of nations'. Only a constitutional community committed to *universal* values such as human dignity could be considered reason-based.

Kant's idea of perpetual peace brought about by reason reaches its climax in his call for unconditional hospitality, which would give every person the right to reside in a foreign country. The stranger could stay there without facing any hostility 'as long as the stranger behaves peacefully where he happens to be'.[11] No one, Kant argues, 'has more of a right to be at a given place on earth than anyone else'.[12] Hospitality is not a utopian notion, but rather a mandatory idea of reason: 'As in the previous articles, we are concerned here with *right*, not with philanthropy, and in this context *hospitality* (a host's conduct to his guest) means the right of a stranger not to be treated in a hostile manner by another upon his arrival on the other's territory.'[13] Hospitality is 'no fantastic or exaggerated conception of right. Rather it is a necessary supplement to the unwritten code of constitutional and international right, for public human right in general, and hence for perpetual peace. Only under this condition can one flatter oneself to be continually progressing toward perpetual peace.'[14]

Hospitality is the highest expression of a universal reason that has come into its own. Reason does not exercise any homogenizing power. Its *friendliness* enables it to acknowledge the Other in their otherness and welcome them. *Friendliness means freedom.*

In addition to reason, the idea of hospitality also displays something universal. For Nietzsche, it is an expression of the 'over-abundant soul'. It is capable of harbouring all singularities within itself: 'And let all that is becoming roaming searching fleeing be welcome here! Henceforth the friendship of hospitality will be my only friendship.'[15] Hospitality promises reconciliation. Its aesthetic manifestation is beauty: 'We are always rewarded in the end for our good will, our patience, our fair-mindedness and gentleness with what is strange, as it gradually casts off its veil and presents itself as a new and indescribable beauty. That is *its thanks* for our hospitality.'[16] The politics of beauty is the politics of hospitality. Xenophobia is hatred, and ugly. It is an expression of a lack of universal reason, a sign that society is still in an unreconciled state. How civilized a society is can be judged by its hospitality in particular, indeed its *friendliness*. *Reconciliation means friendliness*.

3

The Terror of Authenticity

There is much talk of authenticity today. Like all of neoliberalism's advertisements, it appears in an emancipatory guise. To be authentic means to be free of pre-formed expressive and behavioural patterns dictated from the outside. It prescribes that one must equal only oneself and define oneself only through oneself – indeed, that one must be the author and creator of oneself. The imperative of authenticity develops a self-directed compulsion, a compulsion to constantly question oneself, eavesdrop on oneself, stalk and besiege oneself. It thus intensifies narcissistic self-reference.

The compulsion to authenticity forces the I to *produce itself*. Authenticity is ultimately the self's neoliberal form of production; it makes every person the producer of themselves. The I as its own entrepreneur *produces itself, performs itself* and offers itself as a commodity. Authenticity is a selling point.

The striving for authenticity, the striving to equal only oneself, leads to a constant comparison with others. The logic of comparison transforms otherness into sameness, and thus the authenticity of otherness consolidates social conformity: it only permits system-compatible differences, namely diversity. 'Diversity' as a neoliberal term is a resource that can be exploited. Hence it contrasts with *alterity*, which eludes any economic utilization.

Today, everyone wants to be different from others. However, this will to be different enables a continuation of the Same; we are now dealing with a higher-order conformity. Sameness asserts itself by going through otherness; the authenticity of otherness even perpetuates conformity more efficiently than repressive equalization, which is far more fragile.

Socrates as a beloved person is called *atopos* by his students. The Other whom I desire is *placeless*; they elude all comparisons. In *A Lover's Discourse: Fragments*, Roland Barthes writes the following about the atopia of the Other: 'Being Atopic, the other makes language indecisive: one cannot speak of the other, about the other; every attribute is false, painful, erroneous, awkward [. . .].'[1] Socrates as an object of desire is incomparable and singular. Singularity is something entirely different from authenticity. Authenticity presupposes comparability; someone who is authentic is different from others. But Socrates is *atopos*, incomparable. He differs not only from other people, but also from everything else that is different from other people.

The culture of constant comparison does not allow

the negativity of the *atopos*. It makes everything comparable, that is, the same. Thus it renders the experience of the atopic Other impossible. Consumer society strives to eliminate atopic otherness in favour of consumable, indeed heterotopic differences. In contrast to atopic otherness, difference is a positivity. The terror of authenticity as a neoliberal form of production and consumption does away with atopic otherness. The negativity of the entirely Other gives way to the positivity of the Same, in fact the *same Other*.

As a neoliberal production strategy, authenticity creates commodifiable differences. It thus increases the diversity of the commodities in which authenticity is materialized. Individuals express their authenticity primarily through consumption. The imperative of authenticity does not lead to the formation of an autonomous, self-possessed individual; rather, it is entirely co-opted by commerce.

The imperative of authenticity engenders a narcissistic compulsion. Narcissism is distinct from healthy self-love, which has nothing pathological about it; it does not rule out love for the Other. The narcissist, however, is blind to the Other. The Other is bent into shape until the ego recognizes itself in them. The narcissistic subject perceives the world only in shadings of itself. This results in a disastrous consequence: the Other disappears. The boundary between the self and the Other becomes blurred. The self diffuses and becomes diffuse. The I drowns in the self. For a stable self only comes about in the face of the Other; but excessive, narcissistic self-reference creates a feeling of emptiness.

Today, libidinous energies are invested primarily in the ego. The narcissistic accumulation of the ego-libido causes a depletion of the object-libido, that is, the libido that occupies the object. The object-libido creates an object attachment that conversely stabilizes the ego. An excessive narcissistic build-up of the ego-libido causes illness. It produces negative feelings such as fear, shame, guilt and emptiness:

> But it is quite a different thing when a particular, very energetic process forces a withdrawal of libido from objects. Here the libido that has become narcissistic cannot find its way back to objects, and this interference with the libido's mobility certainly becomes pathogenic. It seems that an accumulation of narcissistic libido beyond a certain amount is not tolerated.[2]

Fear results when there is no longer any object charged with libido. The world thus becomes empty and senseless. Owing to the lack of object attachment, the ego is thrown back on itself and broken by itself. Depression is attributable to a narcissistic accumulation of ego-libido.

Freud even applies his libido theory to biology. Cells that only behave narcissistically, that lack eros, endanger the organism's survival. The survival of the cells also requires those cells that behave altruistically, or even sacrifice themselves for others:

> (Perhaps we may also use the term 'narcissistic' in the same sense to describe the cells of malignant neoplasms that destroy the organism. After all, pathologists are prepared to accept that the seeds of these growths are present at birth, and to concede that they display features characteristic of embryos.) All of this being so, it

would appear that the libido of our sexual drives is one and the same thing as the Eros evoked by poets and philosophers, the binding force within each and every living thing.[3]

Eros alone animates the organism. The same applies to society; excessive narcissism de-stabilizes it.

The lack of self-esteem that underlies self-harm, the act of cutting oneself, points to a general crisis of gratification in our society. I cannot produce self-esteem myself; I must rely on the Other as a gratifying authority who loves, praises, acknowledges and appreciates me. The narcissistic isolation of human beings, the instrumentalization of the Other and total competition destroy the climate of gratification. To have a stable self-esteem, I am dependent on the notion that I am important for other people, that I am loved by them. It may be diffuse, but it is indispensable for the feeling of *being* important. It is precisely the insufficient sense of being that is responsible for self-harm. Cutting oneself is not only a ritual of self-punishment for one's own feelings of inadequacy that are typical of today's performance- and optimization-oriented society, but also a cry for love.

The sense of emptiness is a basic symptom of depression and borderline personality disorder. Borderliners are often unable to feel themselves; only when they cut themselves do they feel anything. For the depressive performance subject, the self is a heavy burden. It is tired of itself. Entirely incapable of stepping outside itself, it becomes absorbed in itself, which paradoxically results in an emptying and erosion of the self. Isolated in its mental enclosure, trapped in itself, it loses any connection to the

Other. I touch myself, but I only feel myself through the Other's touch. The Other is instrumental in the formation of a stable self.

The elimination of all negativity is a hallmark of contemporary society. Everything is smoothed out. Communication, too, is smoothed out into an exchange of pleasantries; negative feelings such as sorrow are denied any language, any expression. Every form of injury by others is avoided, yet it rises again as self-harm. Here, too, we find a confirmation of the general logic that the expulsion of the Other results in a process of self-destruction.

According to Alain Ehrenberg, the success of depression is based on a lost connection to conflict. Today's culture of performance and optimization does not allow us to work through conflicts, which is time-consuming. Today's performance subject only knows two states: functioning or failing. In this, there is a resemblance to the condition of machines: machines also know no conflict. They either function correctly or are broken.

Conflicts are not destructive; they have a constructive side. It is only from conflicts that stable relationships and identities ensue. A person grows and matures by working through conflict. The seductive aspect of cutting oneself is that it quickly releases accumulated destructive tension without the time-consuming act of working through conflict. The fast relief of tension is handed over to chemical processes; endogenous drugs are released. It works in a comparable manner to antidepressants: these too suppress states of conflict and quickly restore the depressive performance subject to a functioning state.

The addiction to selfies also has little to do with self-love. It is nothing other than the idle motion of the lonely subject. Faced with one's inner emptiness, one vainly attempts to *produce oneself*. The emptiness merely reproduces itself. Selfies are the self in empty forms; selfie addiction heightens the feeling of emptiness. It results not from self-love, but from narcissistic self-reference. Selfies are pretty, smooth surfaces of an empty, insecure self. To escape this torturous emptiness today, one reaches either for the razorblade or the smartphone. Selfies are smooth surfaces that hide the empty self for a short while. But if one turns them over one discovers their other side, covered in wounds and bleeding. Wounds are the flipsides of selfies.

Could suicide attacks be perverse attempts to feel oneself, to restore a destroyed self-esteem, to bomb or shoot away the burden of emptiness? Could one compare the psychology of terror to that of the selfie and self-harm, which also act against the empty ego? Might terrorists have the same psychological profile as the adolescents who harm themselves, who turn their aggression towards themselves? Unlike girls, boys are known to direct their aggression outwards, against others. The suicide attack would then be a paradoxical act in which auto-aggression and aggression towards others, self-production and self-destruction, become one: a higher-order aggression that is simultaneously *imagined* as the ultimate selfie. The push of the button that sets off the bomb is like the push of the camera button. Terrorists inhabit the imaginary because reality, which consists of discrimination and hopelessness, is no longer worth living. Reality denies them any gratification. Thus they invoke God as an imaginary gratifying authority, and can also be sure that their photograph will be all over the media like a form of selfie directly after the

25

deed. The terrorist is a narcissist with an explosive belt that makes those who wear it especially authentic. Karl-Heinz Bohrer is not wrong when he notes in his essay 'Authenticity and Terror' that terrorism is the final act of authenticity.[4]

4

Anxiety

Anxiety has highly varied aetiologies. It is first of all the foreign, the uncanny, the unknown that triggers anxiety. According to Heidegger, it awakens in the face of a *Nothing*, which is experienced as that which is entirely other than beings. The negativity, the fathomlessness of nothingness, is alien to us today, for the world, as a department store, is filled with beings.

In *Being and Time*, anxiety ensues where the 'at-home of publicness', 'the way things have been publicly interpreted', namely the edifice of familiar everyday patterns of perception and behaviour, collapses and gives way to a 'not-at-home'. It pulls 'Dasein', Heidegger's ontological term for humans, out of the familiar, accustomed 'everydayness', out of social conformism.[1] In anxiety, Dasein is confronted with the uncanny.

The 'they' [*das Man*] embodies social conformity; it

27

prescribes how we are to live, to act, to perceive, to think and to judge: 'We take pleasure and enjoy ourselves as *they* take pleasure; we read, see and judge about literature and art as *they* see and judge; [. . .] we find "shocking" what *they* find shocking.'[2] The dictatorship of the 'they' alienates Dasein from its 'ownmost potentiality-for-Being', from 'authenticity' [*Eigentlichkeit*]:[3] 'When Dasein, tranquillized, and "understanding" everything, thus compares itself with everything, it drifts along towards an alienation in which its ownmost potentiality-for-Being is hidden from it.'[4] The collapse of the familiar horizon of understanding gives rise to anxiety. Only in anxiety does the possibility of Dasein's ownmost potentiality-for-Being disclose itself to it.

What dominates today is not the *uniformity* of 'every Other is like the next' that characterizes the 'they'. That uniformity gives way to the *diversity* of opinions and options. Diversity only permits differences that conform to the system; it constitutes an otherness that has been made consumable. And it perpetuates the Same more efficiently than uniformity does, for its apparent, superficial variety obscures the systemic violence of the Same. Variety and different options create the illusion of an otherness that, in reality, does not exist.

Heidegger's *Eigentlichkeit* is something entirely different from authenticity; in fact, it is the opposite. In the terminology of *Being and Time*, today's authenticity would be a form of *Uneigentlichkeit*. *Eigentlichkeit* precedes the collapse of everydayness. Torn out of the reassuring they-world, Dasein is confronted with the uncanniness of the not-at-home. The authenticity of otherness, on the other hand, takes place within the order of everydayness.

28

The authentic self is a *commodity form of the self*. It realizes itself through consumption.

For Heidegger, anxiety is closely connected to death. Death is not simply the end of Being, but rather 'a way to be',[5] namely the outstanding possibility to be the self. Dying means: "'I am," which means that I will be my ownmost I.'[6] In the face of death, a 'reticent resoluteness that exacts anxiety of itself'[7] chooses *eigentlich* self-Being. Death is *my* death.

Even after Heidegger's so-called 'turn', which marked a radical caesura in his thought, death continues to mean more than simply the end of life. However, it no longer evokes an emphasis on the self; now it stands for the negativity of the abyss, the mystery. 'The task is to draw death into Dasein so that Dasein might be mastered in its abyssal breadth.'[8] The later Heidegger also refers to death as the 'shrine of the Nothing, of that which in every respect is never something that merely exists, but which nevertheless presences, even as the mystery of *Being* itself'.[9] Death inscribes into the beings the negativity of the mystery, of the abyss, of the complete Other.

In our time, which strives to banish all negativity from life, death too falls silent. It no longer *speaks*. It is deprived of all language. It is no longer 'a way to be', but rather no more than the mere end of life, which must be delayed by all means. Death simply means de-production, the end of production. Today, production has totalized itself to become the only way of life. The hysteria over health is ultimately the hysteria of production. Yet it destroys true vitality. The proliferation of healthiness is as obscene as the proliferation of obesity. It is a sickness; morbidity inheres in it. If one denies death for the sake of life, life itself turns into something destructive. It becomes *self-destructive*. Here, too, one finds a confirmation of the dialectic of violence.

It is precisely negativity that enlivens. It nourishes the life of the spirit. The spirit only gains its truth when, in utter fragmentation, it finds itself. Only the negativity of rupture and pain keeps the spirit alive. The spirit 'is this power, not as something positive which closes its eyes to the negative'; it is this power 'only by looking the negative in the face, and dwelling on it'.[10] Today, we flee desperately from the negative instead of dwelling on it. Holding on to the positive, however, only reproduces the Same. There is not only a hell of negativity, but also a hell of positivity. Terror originates not only from the negative, but also from the positive.

The anxiety triggered by the collapse of the familiar world is a *profound anxiety*. It is the same as that profound boredom. Shallow boredom is characterized by a restless 'fidgeting that is directed outward'.[11] In profound boredom, however, the existent in the whole slips from our grasp. But this 'failure', according to Heidegger, contains an 'announcing', a 'calling', that urges Dasein to resolve to take 'action here and now'.

Profound boredom leads to a dawning of those possibilities for action which can seize Dasein, but which would lie idle precisely when *one is bored*.[12] It *calls upon* Dasein to seize its ownmost potentiality-for-Being, that is, to act. It has an *invocatory character*. It *speaks*. It has a *voice*. Today's boredom, which goes hand in hand with hyperactivity, is speechless, mute. It is eliminated by the next activity. Being-active is not yet *action*, however.

In late Heidegger, anxiety stems from the ontologi-

30

cal difference, the difference between Being and beings. Thinking must endure the abyssal *Being without beings* in order to enter a 'yet unentered space'. In a sense, Being precedes beings and makes each appear in a particular light.[13] Thinking 'loves' the 'abyss'; a 'lucid courage for essential anxiety'[14] inheres in it. Without this anxiety, the Same continues. Thinking exposes itself to the 'silent voice' that 'attunes us toward the horror of the abyss'.[15] Horror frees it from *benumbedness by the existent*, in fact *benumbedness by the Same*. It is akin to that 'suffering in which the essential otherness of beings reveals itself in opposition to the tried and usual'.[16]

Today an *ontological indifference* prevails. Both thinking and life blind themselves to their *immanent level*. If there is no contact with it, the *Same* persists. Heidegger's 'Being' refers to this immanent level. It is the level of Being from which thinking starts anew. Only in contact with it can something entirely Other begin. This is also what Deleuze means when he states, 'Quite literally, I will say: they play the fool. Playing the fool. Playing the fool has always been a function of philosophy.'[17] 'Playing the fool' means breaking with the predominant, with the Same. It opens up that virgin immanent level and makes thinking receptive to *truth*, to the *event*, which opens up a new relationship with reality. Then everything appears in a very different light. Only by passing through anxiety can one reach the immanent level of Being. It frees thinking from the pressure of intraworldly beings, from that benumbedness by the Same which Heidegger calls 'forgetfulness of being' [*Seinsvergessenheit*]. That immanent level of Being is virginal; it does not yet have a name: 'But if the human being is to find his way once again into

31

the nearness of being he must first learn to exist in the nameless.'[18]

Today's anxiety has an entirely different aetiology: it stems neither from the collapse of everyday conformity nor abyssal Being. Rather, it takes place within the everyday consensus. It is an *everyday* fear. Its subject remains the 'they':

> The ego orients itself by the others and spins out of control when it no longer believes it can keep up. [. . .] The thought of what the others think of oneself, and what they think that others think of them, thus becomes a source of social anxiety. It is not the objective situation that burdens and breaks the individual so much as the feeling of drawing the short straw compared to significant others.[19]

Heidegger's Dasein, which resolutely strives for its ownmost potentiality-for-Being, for *eigentlich* self-Being, is guided not from without but from within. It resembles a gyrocompass, with an inner centre and a strong orientation towards its ownmost potentiality-for-Being. In this, it is the opposite of distracted radar-humans, who lose themselves outwards.[20] Inward orientation renders superfluous the constant comparisons with other people to which humans guided from without are compelled.

Today, many people are plagued with diffuse fears: fear of failure, fear of falling behind, fear of making a mistake or the wrong decision, fear of not meeting one's own standards. This anxiety is reinforced by a constant comparison with others. It is a *lateral anxiety*, in contrast to the *vertical anxiety* which awakens when faced with the entirely Other, the uncanny, the Nothing.

We live today in the neoliberal system, which breaks down temporally stable structures, fragments living-time and permits the disintegration of what binds us together in the interests of increasing productivity. This neoliberal politics of time creates anxiety and insecurity. And neo-liberalism fragments humans into isolated entrepreneurs of themselves. This isolation, which goes hand in hand with the elimination of solidarity and total competition, produces anxiety. The diabolical logic of neoliberalism is this: *anxiety increases productivity.*

5

Thresholds

Anxiety also awakens on the threshold; it is a typical thresh-old feeling. The threshold is a transition to the unknown. Beyond the threshold, a completely different state of being begins. Thus death is always inscribed in the threshold. In all rites of passages, one dies a death in order to be reborn beyond the threshold. Here death is experienced as a tran-sition: whoever crosses the boundary subjects themselves to a transformation. As a place of transformation, the threshold *hurts*. The negativity of pain inheres in it: 'If you feel the pain of thresholds, you are not a tourist; the transi-tion can occur.'[1] In our time, a threshold-based *transition* gives way to a threshold-less *transit*. On the internet we are tourists more than ever. We no longer inhabit thresh-olds as *homo doloris*. Tourists do not have experiences that imply a transformation, a pain. Thus they remain the *same*. They travel through the hell of sameness.

Thresholds can shock or frighten. But they can also delight or enchant. They stimulate *fantasies for Others*. The compulsion to accelerate the global circulation of capital, communication and information breaks thresholds down and results in a threshold-less, smooth space with an extremely accelerated internal rotation. This is where a new anxiety develops, an anxiety that is completely disconnected from the negativity of the Other.

Digital communication as a new form of production rigorously abolishes all distance in order to become faster. Every protective distance is thus lost. In hypercommunication, everything is mixed with everything else. The boundaries between inside and outside become increasingly permeable. Today, we are completely de-externalized into a 'pure surface', exposed to the incoming rays of all 'influent networks'.[2]

This forced transparency eliminates every gap of vision and information, handing everything over to complete visibility. It causes all spaces of retreat and protection to disappear; thus everything moves threateningly close to us. There is nothing to shield us. We ourselves become no more than transits amid the global network. Transparency and hypercommunication deprive us of any protective inwardness. Indeed, we relinquish them voluntarily and expose ourselves to digital webs that penetrate, illuminate and perforate us. Digital over-exposure and nakedness create a latent fear that stems not from the negativity of the Other, but rather from the excess of positivity. The transparent hell of sameness is not devoid of fear; what is frightening is precisely the increasingly strong *roaring of the Same*.

6

Alienation

Albert Camus's novel *The Outsider*[1] describes the experience of foreignness as the fundamental feeling that defines
being and existence. Humans are strangers to the world,
strangers to other humans and even strangers to themselves. The protagonist, Meursault, is separated from the
Others by a speech-grille. Foreignness expresses itself as
speechlessness. Each person is imprisoned in a cell, separated from Others by a speech-grille. This foreignness
belongs neither in today's age of hypercommunication,
nor in the world as a comfort zone or a department
store.

Paul Celan's poem 'Speech-Grille' [*Sprachgitter*] also
deals with the experience of foreignness:

(Were I like you. Were you like me.
Did we not stand

36

under *one* tradewind.
We are strangers.)

The tiles. Upon them,
close together, the two
heart-grey pools:
two
mouthfuls of silence.[2]

Today we abandon ourselves to a boundless communication. We are almost benumbed by digital hypercommunication. But the noise of communication does not make us any less lonely. Perhaps it even makes us lonelier than speech-grilles do. After all, beyond the speech-grille there is at least a *you*; it still preserves the *closeness of distance*. Hypercommunication, however, destroys both the *you* and *closeness*. *Relationships* are replaced by *connections*. Gaplessness supplants closeness. *Two mouthfuls of silence* might contain more closeness, more language than hypercommunication. Silence is language, but the noise of communication is not.

Today, we are settling into a comfort zone from which the negativity of the foreign has been eliminated. The 'like' is its solution. The digital screen increasingly shields us from the negativity of the foreign, the uncanny. Foreignness is now unwelcome to the extent that it hinders the acceleration of the circulation of information and capital. The compulsion to accelerate levels everything out into the Same. The *transparent* space of hypercommunication is a space without secrets, foreignness or mysteries.

The Other as alienation likewise disappears. Today's

37

working conditions can no longer be described in terms of Marx's theory of alienation. Alienation from labour means that, for the workers, the product of their work is an alien object. They identify neither with their product nor their activity. The more wealth the workers produce, the poorer they become. Their products are snatched away from them. The workers' activity causes their own derealization: 'So much does labour's realization appear as a loss of reality that the worker loses reality to the point of starving to death.'[3] The more they exert themselves, the more they are dominated by the exploitative Other. Marx compares this power relationship, which leads to alienation and derealization, with religion:

> The more man puts into God, the less he retains in himself. The worker puts his life into the object; but now his life no longer belongs to him but to the object. Hence, the greater this activity, the greater is the worker's lack of objects. Whatever the product of his labour, he is not. Therefore the greater his product, the less is he himself.[4]

Because of the alienation in working conditions, it is impossible for the worker to realize themselves. Their work is a continuous *self-derealization*.

Today, we live in a post-Marxist age. In the neoliberal regime, exploitation no longer takes place as alienation and self-derealization, but as freedom, as self-realization and self-optimization. Here there is no Other as an exploiter, forcing me to work and alienating me from myself; rather, I voluntarily exploit myself in the belief that I am realizing myself. This is the diabolical logic of neoliberalism. Hence the first stage of a burnout is euphoria: I plunge into work euphorically until I finally collapse. I realize myself to death. I optimize myself to death. Neoliberal domination hides behind the illusion of freedom. The domination is complete at the moment when it coincides with freedom. This feeling of freedom is disastrous insofar as it does not enable any resistance, any revolution. Where should resistance direct itself? There are no longer any Others from whom any repression originates. Jenny Holzer's truism 'Protect me from what I want' is an apt summary of this paradigm shift.

A new form of alienation is coming into existence today. It is no longer an alienation from the world or from work, but rather a destructive self-alienation: *alienation from oneself*. This self-alienation takes place precisely in the course of self-optimization and self-realization. As soon as the performance subject perceives itself, for example its own body, as a functional object to be optimized, it gradually becomes alienated from it. Owing to the lack of negativity, this self-alienation continues unnoticed. It is not only self-exploitation that has self-destructive effects, but also self-alienation, which expresses itself pathologically as a disorder of the body image. Anorexia, bulimia and binge-eating disorder are symptoms of an increasing self-alienation. By the end, one no longer feels one's own body.

7

Counter-body

The word 'object' comes from the Latin verb *obicere*, which means 'throw at', 'put towards' or 'reproach'. Hence the object is primarily an *Against*, something that turns against me, throws itself at me, opposes me, contradicts me, goes against me and offers resistance. Therein lies its negativity. This level of meaning is still present in the French and English word 'objection', which also denotes disagreement or contradiction.

The experience of a present person as an *obicere* is probably more primal than the *image* of that person as an object. In the image, the imagining subject takes control of the imagined object. It *places* it *alongside itself*. Here the object forfeits much of the negativity of the *against*. The commodity as an object of consumption entirely lacks the negativity of the *obicere*. As a commodity it does not reproach me, does not accuse me, does not oppose me.

40

Instead, it seeks to flatter and please me, to elicit a 'like' from me. The absence of Against and Opposite characterizes today's mode of perception. The world is increasingly losing the negativity of the Against. The digital medium hastens this development. The digital order is the opposite of the terrestrial order, the order of the Earth. Heidegger's late philosophy in particular is concerned with the earthly order; time and again, he invokes the 'gravity of the mountains and the hardness of their primeval rock'.[1] He also speaks of the 'heavy sled' of the 'young farmboy', the 'resistance of the towering firs against the storm' or the 'steep slope opposite'. *Heaviness* and the *Against* dominate the earthly order. The digital, on the other hand, lacks any *heaviness that weighs against us*. It does not appear as an unruly, rebellious, resistant counterpart.[2]

Images, too, are increasingly losing the character of the counterpart. Digital images lack any magic, any enchantment, any seduction. They are no longer *counter-images* with a *life of their own*, a *force of their own*, that confuse, bewitch, perplex or intoxicate the viewer. The 'like' is the absolute zero grade of *perception*.

For Heidegger, the thing [*Ding*] is something that conditions [*be-dingt*] us. Today, this *conditionality* no longer constitutes our sense of being. Handke, too, resolutely opposes the increasing disappearance of the thing and the body in our world. His winter journey to the Danube, Sava, Morava and Drina rivers is very much about the *recuperation of things*. Handke elevates the heavy Serbian shop door to a cipher for the authentic thing. It *throws* its weight *at* us. It is an *object*, an *obicere*. The weight of things constitutes the *weight of the world*. They are *counter-bodies*.

41

The 'pushing of the ancient steel door handle' and the 'shop door that is almost laborious to push open' even trigger a feeling of happiness in Handke:

> The gentle resistance of the thing, caused by age and material weight, its friction with the body of the entrant, reveals an independent counter-body. [. . .] The Serbian shop door is literally an ob-ject, it stands facing us; [. . .] part of a momentary, intense communication of bodies, indeed the subject of a spatial and concrete event that has substance in itself [. . .]. This gentle resistance, the palpable innate force of the simplest things, removes them from the realm of representation, it saves them from disappearing in routine perceptual control.[3]

Handke goes to the market and imagines things as *counter-bodies*. They are all heavy and solid. They rest in themselves. They are 'massive forest-dark honey pots, [. . .] soup chickens as big as turkeys, [. . .] the oddly yellow noodle nests or crowns, [. . .] the often predator-mouthed, often storybook-fat river fish'.[4]

The digital order causes an increasing disembodiment of the world; today, there is less and less communication between bodies. It also does away with counter-bodies by robbing things of their material heaviness, their mass, their own weight, their own life, their own time, and makes them available at all times. Digital objects are no longer an *obicere*. They do not *weigh against* us. No resistance emanates from them. The disappearance of the *Against* now occurs at every level. The 'like' is the opposite of the *obicere*; today, everything craves one. The total absence of the Against is no ideal state, for

42

without an Against one falls hard on oneself. It leads to an *auto-erosion.*

Today, we are also losing the *counterpart* in a particular sense. For Heidegger, the object and the counterpart are not identical. The Greeks would never have experienced that which is present as an object, but rather as a counterpart. With the object, the Against – the *ob-* – is constituted by the subject which it imagines. Thus it takes control of the object. In the counterpart, however, the Against forms in that which 'comes over the perceiving, viewing-hearing human, over those who have never conceived of themselves as a subject for an Object'.[5] The present as a counterpart is not that which 'a subject throws forth as an Object; rather, it is what accrues to perceiving and what human viewing and hearing hold up and portray *as* what has come over it'.[6] This would mean that the ancient Greeks experienced the most uncanny and enchanting counterpart in the presencing of the gods as they gazed into the world. It takes place as an *encounter* with the *entirely Other*. It is thus in the *gaze* and the *voice* that the entirely Other manifests itself.

43

8

Gaze

Near the beginning of his *Seminar, Book X: Anxiety*,
Jacques Lacan presents a didactic fable, the apologue of
the praying mantis. Lacan is wearing a mask, but he does
not know how it looks. With the mask on his face, he
finds himself opposite a gigantic praying mantis. He has
no idea whatsoever what the praying mantis sees, and
thus what effect the sight of the mask will have on it.
Nor is it possible to communicate with this counterpart
through language. He is thus completely at the mercy of
the insect, of its gaze. The fact that the female devours
the male after mating makes it even more daunting. The
entirely Other, which eludes any prediction or calculation
and instils fear, manifests itself as a *gaze*.

With his didactic fable of the praying mantis, Lacan
refers to a scene in *Thomas the Obscure* by Maurice
Blanchot, in which the protagonist is described as a pos-

sessed reader who is devoured by the word as if by a praying mantis. To read means to be *gazed at*:

> In relation to every symbol, he was in the position of the male praying mantis about to be devoured by the female. They looked at each other [*L'un et l'autre se regardaient*]. [...] Thomas slipped toward these corridors, approaching them defencelessly until the moment he was perceived by the very quick of the word. Even this was not fearful, but rather an almost pleasant moment he would have wished to prolong. [...] It was with pleasure that he saw himself in this eye looking at him.[1]

Blanchot here describes a special experience of alienation in which one relinquishes the *supremacy of the eye* and surrenders to the *gaze of the Other*.

The closing scene of *La Dolce Vita* shows a group of bleary-eyed partygoers going to the beach at dawn and observing a giant manta ray being hauled out of the water. The camera shows a close-up of the ray's large, inscrutable eye. Marcello mumbles to himself, 'And it keeps staring at me' (*E questo insiste a guardare*). Jacques Lacan addresses this key scene a number of times. In his seminar 'The Ethics of Psychoanalysis' he portrays the ray that *gazes at one* as a ghastly 'thing':

> [A]t the moment when early in the morning among the pines on the edge of the beach, the jetsetters suddenly begin to move again after having remained motionless and almost disappearing from the vibration of the light; they begin to move toward some goal that pleased

a great many of you, since you associated it with my famous Thing, which in this instance is some disgusting object that has been caught by a net in the sea.[2]

For Lacan, the 'thing' is a *stain*, a *blemish* that *exceeds the picture, the representation*. It constitutes a rupture, a fissure within the established codes of action or perception that constitute the 'symbolic'. It belongs to the 'real', which eludes all representation, all imagining. The thing is a stain, a detail that stands out from the frame, from the symbolic order; the symbolic order is the narration I narrate to *myself*. The thing exceeds this diegetic, narrative framework. It is *the entirely Other* which *gazes at* one. Thus it triggers fear: 'This is what regards us over and above anything else, and shows how anxiety emerges in vision at the locus of the desire that the *a* controls.'[3]

In his film *Rear Window*, Hitchcock stages the triumph of the gaze over the eye.[4] The wheelchair-bound photographer Jeff revels in his enjoyment of the pictures he can see through the window. The uncanny gaze from the other side of the courtyard soon destroys this pleasurable view. Thorwald, whom Jeff suspects of murdering his wife, suddenly notices that Jeff is watching him. When Thorwarld's gaze reaches Jeff, it puts an end to the supremacy of the voyeuristic eye. From this moment, reality is no longer a picture, a pleasurable sight; now Jeff is completely at the mercy of *the Other's gaze*. Thorwald is the counter-figure of the photographer, whose task is to transform reality into a picture, a pleasurable sight. Thorwald's gaze is the *stain* that stands out from the picture. It embodies *the Other's gaze*. Finally, he breaks into Jeff's home. Jeff tries to dazzle him with his camera flash

– that is, to destroy his *gaze*, to banish the uncanny to the picture once more – but fails. The triumph of the gaze over the eye is complete when Thorwald throws Jeff out of the window that previously offered pleasurable sights. Jeff *falls out of the picture entirely* and falls back down to earth: at that moment, *Rear Window* is transformed into *Real Window*.

For Sartre, too, the Other announces their presence as the *gaze*. Sartre does not limit the gaze to the human eye; rather, *being gazed upon* is the central aspect of Being-in-the-world. *World is gaze.* Even the rustling of branches, a half-open window or the slight movement of a curtain is perceived as a gaze.[5] Today the world is sorely lacking in gaze. We rarely feel gazed upon or exposed to a gaze. The world presents itself as a pleasurable sight that seeks to *please* us. The digital screen also lacks any quality of gaze. *Windows* is a *window with no view.* What it does is precisely to shield us from the gaze.

One symptom of paranoia is to suspect gazes everywhere, to feel gazed upon from every corner. This distinguishes it from depression. Paranoia is not a defining sickness of our time, for it is tied to the *negativity of the Other*. A depressive person inhabits a gazeless space in which no experience of the Other is possible.

In Lars von Trier's film *Melancholia*, Justine is cured of her depression at the moment when a desire for the Other awakens in her. Von Trier makes the blue planet in the night sky seem like a *gaze of the Other* which *gazes upon* Justine. It arouses an erotic desire in her. The Other's gaze frees her from depression and changes her into a lover.

Nowadays, the gaze is disappearing at many levels.

47

Domination also takes place without the gaze. Bentham's Panopticon is based on the dominance of the gaze. Its inmates are completely exposed to the overseer's gaze. The observation tower is constructed in such a way that the overseer can see everything without being seen himself: 'The Panopticon is a machine for dissociating the see/being seen dyad: in the peripheric ring, one is totally seen, without ever seeing; in the central tower, one sees everything without ever being seen.'[6] The inmates only see the silhouette of the central tower. They cannot know if they are being observed at any given moment. Thus they feel constantly *gazed upon*, even if the overseer is not present. *The dominance of the gaze rests on a central perspective.*

Orwell's surveillance state likewise establishes a *dominance of the gaze*. Big Brother is omnipresent as the gaze via the telescreens. He sees everything without being seen. *Repression manifests itself as the gaze*:

> The hallway smelt of boiled cabbage and old rag mats. At one end of it a coloured poster, too large for indoor display, had been tacked to the wall. It depicted simply an enormous face, more than a metre wide: the face of a man of about forty-five, with a heavy black moustache and ruggedly handsome features. [. . .] On each landing, opposite the lift shaft, the poster with the enormous face gazed from the wall. It was one of those pictures which are so contrived that the eyes follow you about when you move. BIG BROTHER IS WATCHING YOU, the caption beneath it ran.[7]

What distinguishes the digital medium from the optical one is that it is a *medium with no gaze*. So too the digital

48

panopticon, which would in fact no longer be an *opticon*, does not rely on the gaze, on the central optical perspective. That is precisely why it sees substantially more, and indeed more deeply, than the analogous Panopticon. The distinction between centre and periphery becomes meaningless; the digital panopticon operates aperspectivally. Aperspectival screening is far more efficient than perspectival surveillance because one is illuminated from all sides, even from the inside. Thoughts elude the gaze, but they do not escape the digital panopticon. Big Data has no need for the gaze. Unlike surveillance with a central perspective, aperspectival screening no longer has any blind spots.

The absence of a repressive gaze creates – and this is a decisive difference from the surveillance strategy of the disciplinary society – a deceptive sense of freedom. The inmates of the digital panopticon do not feel *gazed upon*, that is, under surveillance. So they feel free and expose themselves voluntarily. The digital panopticon does not restrict freedom; it exploits it.

9

Voice

The voice comes from *elsewhere*, from the *outside*, from the *Other*. The *voices* one hears elude localization. Derrida's famous arguments on the phonocentrism of Western metaphysics, which see in the voice a privileged place of immediate self-presence and special proximity to meaning, to the *logos*, completely miss the exteriority of the voice. Like the gaze, it is a medium that precisely undermines self-presence, self-transparency, and inscribes the entirely Other, the unknown, the uncanny into the self.

Kafka's stories, for example *Before the Law* or *The Castle*, suggestively stage the negativity, the inaccessibility, the secret of the *entirely Other* which eludes all representation. The *man from the country* waits until his death before the door to the law, yet is never admitted. The law remains closed to him. Nor does the land surveyor K.

gain admittance to the castle. It is no coincidence that the castle first manifests itself as a *voice*. It is the locus of the entirely Other. After his arrival in the village, K. makes a telephone call to the castle. What he hears on the telephone is no intelligible word, no speaking, no discourse, but rather an eerie, unintelligible, *singing voice from the distance*:

> From the mouthpiece came a humming, the likes of which K. had never heard on the telephone before. It was as though the humming of countless childlike voices – but it wasn't humming either, it was singing, the singing of the most distant, of the most utterly distant, voices – as though a single, high-pitched yet strong voice had emerged out of this humming in some quite impossible way and now drummed against one's ears as if demanding to penetrate more deeply into something other than one's wretched hearing. K. listened without telephoning, with his left arm propped on the telephone stand he listened thus.[1]

The voice penetrates the deep layer below the level of consciousness. The gaze has the same intensity and deep effect. The mysterious barmaid Frida has 'a gaze of exceptional superiority'.[2] It penetrates the sphere that eludes conscious actions. It communicates with the Other within the I, with the I as the Other:

> When this gaze descended on K., it seemed to him to be a gaze that had already decided matters concerning him, whose existence he himself still knew nothing about, but of whose existence that gaze now convinced him.[3]

The voice too undermines self-presence. It makes a deep fissure within the subject that allows the entirely Other to irrupt into the self. In the short story *Investigations of a Dog*, Kafka describes an 'awe-inspiring voice which made the forest fall silent'.[4] It makes the listener become *beside himself*:

> And I was, really, completely beside myself. In normal circumstances I would have been gravely ill, incapable of moving, but I couldn't resist the melody, which the dog soon appeared to take over for himself.[5]

For Kafka, the voice is a preferred medium for the Other, the entirely Other. Only a *weakness*, a *metaphysical weakness*, a *primal passivity* makes us receptive for the voice of the Other. In a letter to Milena, Kafka compares the prophets to 'weak children' who 'heard the Voice calling them' and felt 'fear tearing through their brain'.[6] They are *weak* in the face of the *tremendous voice of the Other*. The eroticism of the voice also lies in the fact it prevents the 'psychological subject' from being 'reinforced'. The voice makes it *weak*, and it disappears. The voice causes a 'loss' of the self.[7]

Today, we are no longer *weak children*. Childlike weakness as receptiveness to the Other is not in keeping with the constitution of a narcissistic society. The increasingly strengthened ego, nurtured and exploited by the neoliberal conditions of production, is more and more isolated from the Other. The proliferating ego is entirely impervious to the voice of the Other. The narcissistic overload of self-reference makes us completely deaf and blind to the Other. We no longer perceive the Other's voice amid the digital noise of the Same. We have thus become resistant to voice and gaze.

For Kafka, the voice and the gaze are also *signs of the body*. A communication devoid of these *body signs* is merely an exchange with ghosts:

> How did people ever get the idea they could communicate with one another by letter! One can think about someone far away and one can hold on to someone nearby; everything else is beyond human power. [. . .] Written kisses never arrive at their destination; the ghosts drink them up along the way.[8]

Digital means of communication are far more disembodied than letters. Handwriting is still a body sign; all digital writing is the same. Most of all, digital media elide the Other as a counterpart. They actually rob us of the ability to think about someone far away and to hold on to someone nearby. They replace closeness and distance with gaplessness.

Roland Barthes speaks of the 'grain of the voice' to describe that corporeality of the voice which eludes all forms of representation, both imagining and meaning. This deep bodily layer of the voice does not mean anything, but causes sensual pleasure:

> [. . .] something is there, manifest and stubborn (one hears only *that*), beyond (or before) the meaning of the words [. . .] something which is directly the cantor's body, brought to your ears in one and the same movement from deep down in the cavities, the muscles, the membranes, the cartilages [. . .] as though a single skin

lined the inner flesh of the performer and the music he sings.[9]

Barthes distinguishes between pheno-song and geno-song. The 'grain of the voice' inheres in geno-song, where the concern is not meaning, not the *signified*, but rather the 'voluptuousness of its sound-signifiers'.[10] This pleasure has little to do with meaning. It communicates itself corporeally. The body-related geno-song is erotic, and seduces. This seductive power is absent from the pheno-song, however, which is dedicated to structure, rules, communication, representation and expression: 'here it is the soul which accompanies the song, not the body'.[11] In the pheno-song, neither tongue nor membranes are audible. It only brings out the *sense*, whereas the geno-song puts the *sensual* into sound. The pheno-song lacks any corporeality, any sensuality.

In the geno-song, the concern is to 'patinate' the consonants 'too readily thought to constitute the very armature of our language [. . .] and always prescribed as needing to be "articulated", detached, emphasized *in order to fulfil the clarity of meaning*'.[12] In the geno-song, consonants become 'simply the springboard for the admirable vowels'.[13] Vowels inhabit the voluptuous body; consonants work on the sense. The 'truth' of language lies not in 'its functionality (clarity, expressivity, communication)',[14] however, but in voluptuousness and seduction.

In Novalis, too, consonants stand for prose, meaning and utility. To be 'consonant' means to be inhibited, limited, constrained. The negativity of the unknown, of the mysterious, of the enigma, is alien to the *consonant spirit*. Vowels, by contrast, are seductive, poetic and romantic.

54

Consonants do not permit us to drift into the distance: 'Distant philosophy sounds like poetry – because every call into the distance becomes a vowel.'[15] Today we live in a *consonant time*. Digital communication is a consonant communication. It is devoid of secrets, mysteries and poetry. It abolishes distance in favour of gaplessness and distancelessness.

The schisms in the psychic apparatus that follow the effects of prohibition and repression bring voices into existence. Thus Daniel Paul Schreber, author of *Memoirs of My Nervous Illness*, feels he is being followed about by voices. They sound from an *entirely other place*. Schreber speaks of 'communications from voices originating elsewhere, indicating supernatural origin'.[16] The voices that speak to him incessantly are attributed to God: 'To me therefore it is *unshakable truth*, that God *reveals Himself anew* daily and hourly through the talking of voices.'[17] Schreber uses a symphonion, music boxes and harmonicas and his voice 'to drown the senseless and shameless twaddle of the voices, and so procure temporary rest for my nerves'.[18] The voice is a revenant, a returned spirit. What was excluded and repressed returns as a voice. The negativity of denial and repression is constitutive of the voice; in the voice, the repressed psychic content comes back. In a society where the negativity of repression and denial increasingly gives way to permissiveness and affirmation, ever fewer voices will be heard. The noise of the Same, however, will grow.

The voice often represents a higher authority, a transcendence. It sounds from *above*, from the *entirely Other*. That is why morality often uses the voice as a metaphor. In addition, the voice has an inherent exteriority: the voice of the moral command comes from the inner *exterior*. Already the warning voice that Socrates supposedly heard time and again as a moral authority comes from a *daimon*, from an uncanny other.

Kant's reason also enters the discourse with an imperious voice. Morality consists in rejecting happiness and all sensual inclinations, and submitting completely to the moral law, the 'voice of reason', the 'heavenly voice', which 'makes even the boldest evildoer tremble'.[19] For Heidegger, the voice of reason is replaced by the 'voice of conscience',[20] which calls upon Dasein to seize its 'ownmost potentiality-for-Being'. Here, too, the voice has an inherent exteriority. In one passage from *Being and Time*, Heidegger speaks quite unexpectedly of the 'voice of the friend whom every Dasein carries with it'.[21] Hearing this voice, Heidegger states, 'constitutes the primary and authentic way in which Dasein is open for its ownmost potentiality-for-Being'.[22] Why does the voice come from the friend? Why does Heidegger call upon the friend when he is concerned with the voice in particular? *The friend is the Other.* Heidegger here requires the Other in order to provide the voice with a certain transcendence.

The later Heidegger makes the voice the medium of thinking as such. Thinking exposes itself to a voice, and this voice attunes and determines it:

> This hearing [*Gehör*] has something to do not only with the ear, but also with a human's belonging [*Zugehörigkeit*] to what its essence is attuned to. Humans are at-tuned [*ge-stimmt*] to what determines [*be-stimmt*] their essence. In this attunement humans are touched and called forth

by a voice [*Stimme*] that peals all the more purely, the more it silently reverberates through what speaks.[23]

The voice sounds from without, from the entirely Other to which thinking exposes itself. Voice and gaze are the medium in which Being manifests itself as that which is other than Being, yet attunes and determines it. Thus Heidegger speaks of the 'sameness of heaven's gaze and voice'.[24] Eros is part of thinking as a striving towards the Other: 'The Other, that which is inseparable from my love for you and from my thinking in other respects, is difficult to utter. I call it Eros, the oldest of the gods according to Parmenides. The beating of that god's wings touches me every time I take a substantial step in thinking and venture onto untrodden ground.'[25] Thinking must surrender to the negativity of the Other and proceed into the unknown. Otherwise it degenerates into a positive operation that continues the Same.

For Paul Celan, too, the voice which comes from the Other, from the *you*, is constitutive of literature. Literature begins where language becomes 'voiced'. It starts from the encounter with the Other: 'Does one take, when thinking of poems, does one take such routes with the poems? Are these routes only re-routings, detours from you to you? But they are also at the same time, among many other routes, routes on which language becomes voice, they are encounters, routes of a voice to a perceiving you.'[26]

In the digital echo chamber, where one primarily hears *oneself* speaking, the *voice of the Other* increasingly disappears. Today, the world has been made less *voiced* by the Other's absence. Unlike the *you*, the *it* has no voice. The *it* neither speaks nor gazes at anything. The disappearing *counterpart* makes the world voiceless and gazeless.

Digital communication is highly deficient in gaze and voice. Connections and interconnections are created without the voice or the gaze. In this, they differ from relationships and encounters, which are dependent on the voice and the gaze. They are, in fact, special experiences of the voice and the gaze. They are *bodily experiences*.

The digital medium has a disembodying effect. It robs the voice of its *grain*, its corporeality, indeed the depths of the cavities, muscles, membranes and cartilage. The voice is *smoothed out*. It becomes *transparent* for meaning. Its only content is the *signified*. This smooth, bodiless, transparent voice does not *seduce* or arouse voluptuousness. Seduction rests on the *surplus of signifiers*, which cannot be reduced to the signified. It aims for the 'voluptuousness of its sound-signifiers', which do not *mean* anything; they do not convey any information. Seduction takes place in a space where signifiers circulate without being *confronted* by the signified. The unambiguous signified does not seduce. And the place of voluptuousness is the skin, which is stretched over the meaning. The secret, too, is not simply a concealed, hidden signified waiting to be uncovered, but rather a surplus of signifiers that cannot be dissolved into the signified. It cannot be uncovered; one could say it is the *covering itself*.

10

The Language of the Other

In Jeff Koons's picture series *Easyfun-Ethereal*, all manner of consumer articles are assembled into colourful pictures at the computer. Cupcakes, sausages, grains of corn, underwear and wigs fly through the air, all thrown together. His pictures mirror our society, which has become a department store. It is stuffed full of short-lived objects and advertisements. It has lost all otherness, all foreignness; thus it is no longer possible to marvel at anything. Jeff Koons's art, which merges seamlessly with consumer culture, elevates consumerism to a figure of salvation. The sculpture *Balloon Venus*, with a figure in a birthing position, even gives birth to a new saviour: its belly contains a bottle of champagne, Dom Pérignon Rosé, vintage 2003.

For Adorno, 'estrangement from the world' is an aspect of art. Someone who perceives the world as anything other than foreign is not perceiving it at all. A negative tension is essential to art; for Adorno, there was therefore no such thing as feel-good art. Likewise, estrangement from the world is an aspect of philosophy. It inheres in *spirit* itself. Thus spirit, by its very nature, is *critique*.

In the society of the 'like', everything becomes likeable – art too. Thus we are unlearning wonder:

> The more densely people have spun a categorial web around what is other than subjective spirit, the more fundamentally have they disaccustomed themselves to the wonder of that other and deceived themselves with a growing familiarity with what is foreign. Art hopes to correct this, though feebly and with a quickly exhausted gesture. A priori, art causes people to wonder [. . .].[1]

Today, the world is wrapped in digital webs that permit nothing except subjective spirit. This has created a familiar field of view from which all negativity of the foreign and the Other is eliminated, a digital echo chamber in which subjective spirit encounters nothing but itself. It covers the world in its own retina, as it were.

The digital screen permits no wonder. With increasing familiarity, all traces of the potential for wonder that enlivens our spirit disappear. Art and philosophy are obliged to reverse the betrayal of the foreign, of that which is different from subjective spirit; this means liberating the Other from the categorial web of subjective spirit, restoring to it its *strange*,[2] *wondrous otherness*.

Art is distinguished by a riddle character: 'Ultimately, what lives on in art's riddle character, through which art most abruptly opposes the unquestionable existence of objects of action, is its own riddle.'³ The object of action is a product of the subject of action, which is incapable of wonder. Only 'contemplation without violence', 'distanced nearness',⁴ indeed the *nearness of distance* liberates things from the constraints of the subject of action. Beauty only reveals itself to the long, contemplative gaze. Where the subject of action withdraws, where its blind compulsion to the object is broken, things are given back their otherness, their mysteriousness, their foreignness, their secret.

For Celan, too, art preserves the uncanny. It effects a 'stepping beyond what is human, a stepping into an uncanny realm turned toward the human'.⁵ Art – and herein lies its paradoxical existence – is at home in the uncanny. Literary images are imaginings in an outstanding sense. They are 'imaginings as glimpsable inclusions of the foreign in the sight of the familiar'.⁶ There is a darkness that inheres in poetry, testifying to the presence of the foreign which is guarded within it. It is the darkness 'attributed to the poem, for the sake of an encounter from a – perhaps self-created – distance'.⁷ Poetic imagining, literary imagination, works the foreign into the Same. Without inclusions of the foreign, the Same continues. In the hell of sameness, the poetic imagination is dead. Peter Handke invokes Celan when he notes, 'The great imagination – passes; but provides exploitable inclusions.'⁸ Through its inclusions of the foreign, the imagination de-stabilizes the Same, the *identity of the name*: 'The imagination goes through me (a), transforms me into Nobody (b) and makes me a speaker (c).'⁹ The poet as a nameless, a nobody speaker speaks *in the name of the Other, the entirely Other.*

Art presupposes self-transcendence. Whoever has art in mind is self-forgetful. Art creates an 'I-distance'.[10] Forgetful of itself, it enters the uncanny and unfamiliar: 'Perhaps – I am only asking – perhaps poetry, like art, moves with a self-forgotten I toward the uncanny and strange.'[11] Today, we no longer inhabit the earth poetically; we settle into the digital comfort zone. We are anything but nameless or self-forgetful. The digital web inhabited by the ego has lost all that is foreign, all that is uncanny. The digital order is not poetic; within it, we operate in the numerical space of the Same.

Today's hypercommunication suppresses the free spaces of silence and solitude without which it would have been impossible to say things that were truly worth saying. It suppresses *language*, of which silence is an essential part. It rises from a *silence*; without that, it is already noise. Poetry, according to Celan, shows a 'strong tendency towards silence'. The noise of communication makes it impossible to *listen. Nature* as a poetic principle only reveals itself in a primal passivity of listening: 'Concerning Hyperion's repeated statement on nature, "My entire being falls silent and listens": the being that falls silent is indeed characterized by "listening", not "looking."'[12]

The French writer Michel Butor points to a crisis in contemporary literature and reads it as a crisis of spirit:

Almost nothing has happened in literature during the last ten or twenty years. There are scores of publications, but a spiritual stasis. The cause is a crisis of communication. The new means of communication are admirable, but they are producing an incredible noise.[13]

62

Today, the silent voice of the Other is drowned out by the noise of the Same. The literary crisis ultimately stems from the expulsion of the Other.

Literature and art are on the way to the *Other*. The desire for the Other is their essential trait. In his *Meridian* speech, Celan explicitly relates literature to the Other: 'I think that it had always been part of the poem's hopes to speak [. . .] *on another's behalf* – who knows, perhaps on behalf of *a totally other*.'[14] The poem only takes place in the encounter with an Other, in the secret of the encounter, in the face of a counterpart:

> The poem wants to head toward some other, it needs this other, it needs a counterpart. It seeks it out, it bespeaks itself to it.
>
> Each thing, each human is, for the poem heading toward this other, a figure of this.[15]

Not only every person is a counterpart, but also every thing. The poem invokes a thing, too: it meets it in its otherness; it enters into a dialogical relationship with it. To the poem, everything appears as a *you*.

The counterpart as the presence of the Other is increasingly disappearing from contemporary perception and communication. More and more, the counterpart degenerates into a mirror which mirrors oneself. All attention is focused on the ego. It is surely the task of art and literature to *de-mirror* our perception, to open it up to the counterpart, for the Other – as a person or an object. Today's politics and economy of attention direct this towards the ego; it serves a self-production. It is increasingly withdrawn from the Other and led to the ego. Today, we compete mercilessly for attention. For one another, we are shop windows vying for attention.

Celan's *poetics* of attentiveness is the opposite of today's *economy* of attention. It devotes it exclusively to the Other: 'Attention – permit me to quote here a phrase by Malebranche, via Walter Benjamin's essay on Kafka – "Attention is the natural prayer of the soul."'[16] The soul is always in a position of prayer. It is in search. It is a praying appeal to the Other, the entirely Other. For Lévinas, too, attention means a 'surplus of consciousness' that 'presupposes the call of the other'; to be attentive is to 'recognize the mastery of the other'.[17] Today, the economy of attention overgrows both the poetics and the ethics of attentiveness. It betrays the Other. The economy of attention totalizes the time of the self. The poetics of attentiveness, on the other hand, discovers the time that is most specific to the Other, the *time of the Other*. It 'lets the most essential aspect of the other speak: its time'.[18]

The poem seeks the conversation with the Other: 'The poem becomes [. . .] the poem of someone who – still – perceives, is turned toward phenomena, questioning and addressing these; it becomes conversation – often a desperate conversation.'[19] The poem is a dialogical event. Today's communication is extremely narcissistic. It takes place entirely without a *you*, without any appeal to the Other. In the poem, however, I and you bring forth each other:

> Only in the space of this conversation does the addressed constitute itself, as it gathers around the I addressing and naming it. But the addressed which through naming has, as it were, become a you, brings its otherness into this present.[20]

64

Today's communication does not allow us to say 'you', to appeal to the Other. The appeal to the Other as you presupposes a 'primal distance'.[21] Digital communication in particular is designed to eliminate all distance. Today, by means of digital media, we seek to bring the Other as close as possible. This does not give us more of the Other; rather, it causes them to disappear.

Furthermore, the appeal to the other as a you is not without risks. One must be willing to expose oneself to the otherness and foreignness of the Other. 'You-aspects' of the Other elude all safeguards. They 'pull us dangerously to extremes, loosening the well-tried structure, leaving behind more doubt than satisfaction, shaking up our security – altogether uncanny, altogether indispensable'.[22] Today's communication strives to eliminate those you-aspects from the Other and even them out into an 'it', into the Same.

11

The Thinking of the Other

Self-being does not simply mean being free. The self is also a burden. Self-being is being-burdened-with-oneself. Regarding the burdensome character of self-being, Emmanuel Levinas writes: 'In psychological and anthropological descriptions this is explained by the fact that the I is already riveted to itself, its freedom is not as light as grace but already a heaviness, the ego is irremissibly itself.'[1] The reflexive pronoun '(it)self' (*soi*) means that the I is chained to a heavy, burdensome double, that it must bear a weight, an excessive weight which it cannot let go of for as long as it exists. This existential constitution manifests itself as fatigue. Fatigue 'does not occur simply in a hand that is letting slip the weight it finds tiring to lift, but in one that is holding on to what it is letting slip, even when it has let it drop [. . .].'[2] Depression can be understood as a pathogenic development of this *modern* ontology of the self. It is, as Alain Ehrenberg puts it, *fatigue d'être soi* [tiredness of being oneself]. In the neo-liberal conditions of production, that ontological burden increases to the point of excess. The maximization of the burden ultimately serves the purpose of maximizing productivity.

Heidegger's Dasein never tires. The tireless ability, the emphasis on the ability-to-be-oneself, dominates his ontology of the self. Heidegger even understands death as an outstanding *possibility* to seize the self expressly. In the face of death, an emphatic I-am awakens. For Levinas, consistently enough, death manifests itself as inability-to-be-able, as a radical passivity. It is *impossibility* as such. It becomes visible as the event in whose face the subject gives up all heroism of the self, all ability, all possibility, all initiative: 'There is in the suffering at the heart of which we have grasped this nearness of death – and still at the level of the phenomenon – this reversal of the subject's activity into passivity.'³ The inability-to-be-able in the face of death resembles that relationship with the Other which Levinas terms 'eros'. Eros, he writes, is 'just as with death'. It is a relationship with the Other that 'is impossible to translate into powers'.⁴ It is precisely the passivity of the inability-to-be-able that provides access to the Other.

'To be able' is the quintessential *modal verb of the I*. The totalization of ability that currently enforces the neoliberal conditions of production blinds the I to the Other. It leads to the expulsion of the Other. Burnout and depression are the deserts left behind by destructive ability.

The inability-to-be-able manifests itself as a different fatigue, as a *fatigue for the Other*. It is no longer I-fatigue.

67

Thus Levinas now speaks of *lassitude* rather than *fatigue*. 'Primordial lassitude'[5] refers to a radical passivity which eludes every initiative by the I. It ushers in the *time of the Other*. *Fatigue*, by contrast, stems from the *time of the self*. Primordial fatigue opens up a space that is inaccessible to any ability, any initiative. I am weak in the face of the Other. I am weak for the Other. It is precisely in this *metaphysical weakness* of the inability-to-be-able that a desire for the Other awakens. Only through a rupture in being as self-being, only through a *weakness of being* does the Other announce their presence. Even if the subject has satisfied all its needs, it is in search of the Other. Needs apply to the self; the orbit of desire lies outside the self. It is freed from the gravity of the *oneself*, which pulls the I ever deeper into itself.

Only eros is capable of freeing the I from depression, from narcissistic entanglement in itself. From this perspective, *the Other* is a redemptive formula. Only eros, which pulls me out of myself and towards the Other, can overcome depression. The depressive performance subject is entirely detached from the Other. The desire for the Other, indeed the *calling* or 'conversion' to the Other,[6] would be a metaphysical antidepressant that breaks open the narcissistic shell of the I.

To encounter a human being, according to Levinas, 'is to be kept awake by an enigma'.[7] Today, we have lost this experience of the Other as an enigma or secret. The Other now is entirely subject to the teleology of use, to economic calculation and evaluation. They become *transparent*. They are demoted to an economic object. The *Other as an enigma*, on the other hand, eludes all exploitation.

Love always presupposes otherness – not only the otherness of the Other, but also the otherness of one's own person. The duality of the person is constitutive of love for oneself:

> What is love but understanding and rejoicing at the fact that another lives, acts and feels in a way different from and opposite to ours? If love is to bridge these antitheses through joy it may not deny or seek to abolish them. – Even self-love presupposes an unblendable duality (or multiplicity) in one person.[8]

When all duality is wiped out, one drowns in the self. Without any duality, one merges with oneself. This narcissistic meltdown is fatal. Alain Badiou also calls love the 'stage of the Two'.[9] It enables us to re-create the world from the perspective of the Other and leave behind the habitual. It is an event that allows something entirely Other to begin. Today, on the other hand, we inhabit the *stage of the One*.

Faced with the pathologically enlarged ego bred specially by the neoliberal conditions of production and exploited in order to increase productivity, what is necessary is once more to consider life from the perspective of the Other, of the relationship with the other, and to afford the Other an ethical precedence – indeed, to relearn the language of responsibility, to *listen to the Other and respond*. For Levinas, language as 'saying' (*dire*) is nothing other than 'responsibility of the one for the other'.[10] Today, that 'pre-original language' as the language of the Other is being destroyed by the noise of hypercommunication.

12

Listening

Some time in the future, there may be a profession known as 'listener'. For a fee, the listener gives an ear to the Other. People go to the listener because there is hardly anyone else left who will listen to the Other. Today, we are increasingly losing the ability to listen. It is hampered most of all by the intensifying focus on the ego, by the narcissization of society. Narcissus does not return the loving voice of the nymph Echo, who would really be the voice of the Other. Thus it degenerates into a repetition of his own voice.

Listening is not a passive act. It is distinguished by a special activity: first I must welcome the Other, which means affirming the Other in their otherness. Then I give them an ear. Listening is a bestowal, a giving, a gift. It helps the Other to speak in the first place. It does not passively follow the speech of the Other. In a sense, listening precedes speaking; it is only listening that causes the Other to speak. I am already listening before the Other speaks, or I listen so that the Other will speak. Listening invites the Other to speak; it frees them for their otherness. The listener is a resonance chamber in which the Other *speaks themselves free*. Thus listening can have a healing effect.

Elias Canetti elevates Hermann Broch to an ideal listener, who selflessly *gives* the Other an ear. His hospitable, listening silence invites the Other to *speak themselves free*:

> There was nothing one could not have said, he rejected nothing. One felt ill at ease only as long as one had not expressed oneself fully. While in other such conversations there comes a point where one suddenly says to oneself: 'Stop. This far and no further,' where one senses the danger of relinquishing too much – for how does one find the way back to oneself, and how after that can one bear to be alone? – with Broch there was never such a point or such a moment, one never came up against warning signs, one staggered on, faster and faster, as though drunk. It is devastating to discover how much one has to say about oneself; the further one ventures, the more one loses oneself, the faster the words flow [. . .].[1]

Broch's silence expresses the friendship of hospitality; he retreats entirely to make space for the Other. He becomes all ears, with no mouth to interfere.

Broch's silence is a hospitable silence that differs from the silence of an analyst, who takes in all the information instead of listening to the Other. The hospitable listener empties themselves to become the resonance chamber of the Other, saving the Other to themselves. Simply listening can heal.

The silence of the listener, according to Canetti, is 'punctuated by short, hardly perceptible breaths, which showed not only that one had been listened to but that what one had said had also been *welcomed*, as though with every sentence uttered one had stepped into a house and made oneself elaborately at home'.[2] These small breathing sounds are signs of hospitality, a *reception* that has no need of any judgement. They are a minimum reaction, for 'fully-formed words and sentences would have implied a judgement, would have amounted to taking a position'.[3] Canetti refers to a peculiar 'stillness' that acted as a withholding of judgement. The listener refrains from judgement as if any judgement would amount to a prejudgement, which would be a betrayal of the Other.

The art of listening takes place as an art of breathing. The hospitable welcoming of the Other is an inhalation, yet one that does not absorb the Other, but instead harbours and preserves them. Through the act of emptying oneself, the listener becomes no one. It is this emptiness that distinguishes his friendly behaviour: 'He seemed to assimilate all manner of things in order to preserve them.'[4]

The responsible stance of the listener towards the Other expresses itself as *patience*. The *passivity of patience* is the first maxim of listening. The listener undertakes the unreserved exposure of the self to the Other. *Exposure* is a further maxim of the ethics of listening; it is the only thing preventing us from *pleasing ourselves*. The *ego* is incapable of listening. The space of listening as a reso-

72

nance chamber of the Other opens up where the ego is suspended. The narcissistic ego is replaced with a possession by the other, a desire for the Other.

The listener's care is for the Other – in contrast to Heidegger's care, which is care for oneself. Canetti wishes to listen out of care for Others. It is only through listening that the Other becomes able to speak:

> Most important of all is talking to unknown people. But it has to be done in such a way that they do the talking, and the only thing one does oneself is to get them to talk. When that is no longer possible for a man, then death has begun.[5]

This death is not *my* death but the death of the Other. My speech, my judgement and even my enthusiasm always makes something in the Other die:

> Let everyone speak: do not speak yourself; your words rob people of their own form. Your enthusiasm blurs their boundaries; they no longer know themselves when you speak; they are you.[6]

The culture of the 'like' rejects every form of injury or distress. But anyone who seeks to evade injury completely will experience nothing; the negativity of injury inheres in every deep experience, every deep insight. The mere 'like' is the absolute zero level of experience. Elias Canetti distinguishes between two kinds of mind: 'those that settle in wounds and those that settle in houses'.[7] The wound is the opening through which the Other enters. It is also the ear that keeps itself open for the Other. Someone who is entirely at home with themselves, who locks themselves in their house, is incapable of listening. The house protects the ego from the irruption of the Other. The wound breaks open that domestic, narcissistic inwardness. Thus it becomes an open door for the Other.

In analogue communication we usually have a concrete addressee, a personal counterpart. Digital communication, on the other hand, fosters an expansive, de-personalized communication that has no need of a personal counterpart, no need of a gaze or a voice. We constantly send messages on Twitter, for example. But they are not directed at a concrete person. They *mean* no one. Social media do not necessarily foster a culture of discussion. They are often affect-driven. Shitstorms are an undirected flood of affects that does not form any public discourse.

I obtain information from the web, which does not require me to turn to a personal counterpart. I do not venture into the public space to acquire information or commodities; rather, I have them brought to me. Digital communication connects me, but simultaneously isolates me. It eliminates distance, but gaplessness alone does not create personal closeness.

Without the presence of the Other, communication degenerates into an accelerated exchange of information. It creates no *relationship*, only *connection*. It is a communication with no *neighbour*, without any neighbourly *closeness*. Listening means something entirely different from exchanging information; listening does not involve any exchange whatsoever. Without neighbourliness, without listening, no community can form. *Community is listenership.*

On Facebook, people do not point out problems that we could tackle and discuss together. They mostly post advertisements that require no discussion and merely serve to give the poster a certain profile. In this environment, it is unlikely to occur to someone that the Other might be experiencing worries or pain. In the community of the 'like', one encounters only oneself or like-minded persons. Thus no *discourse* is possible. Political space is a space in which I encounter Others, speak to Others and listen to them.

Listening has a political dimension. It is an act, an active participation in the existence of Others, in their suffering too. It is what joins and connects people to form a community in the first place. Today, we hear a great deal, but are increasingly losing the ability to listen to Others and give an ear to their language, their suffering. Today, everyone is somehow on their own with themselves, with their suffering, with their fears. Suffering is privatized and individualized. Thus it becomes an object of a therapy that tampers with the I, with its psyche. Everyone is ashamed and simply blames themselves for their weakness and inadequacy. No connection is established between my suffering and your suffering. Thus the *sociality of suffering* is overlooked.

Today's strategy for domination is to privatize suffering and fear, and thus conceal its sociality, preventing its *socialization* and *politicization*. Politicization means the translation of the private into the public. Today, by contrast, the public is dissolved into the private. The public sphere disintegrates into private spaces.

The political will to form a public space, a community of listening, the *political listenership*, is radically fading.

Digital interconnection supports this development. The internet manifests itself today not as a space of shared, communicative action. Rather, it disintegrates into exhibition spaces of the I, in which one primarily advertises oneself. Today's internet is nothing but the resonance chamber of the isolated self. An advertisement does not listen.

One can develop an ethics of listening from Michael Ende's novel *Momo*. Momo is characterized first of all by a wealth of time: 'time was Momo's only form of wealth'.[8] Momo's time is a special time. It is the time of the Other, the time that she gives Others by listening to them. Momo is admired for her ability to listen. She appears as a *listener*:

> [. . .] what little Momo was better at than anyone else was *listening*.
>
> Anyone can listen, you may say – what's so special about that? – but you'd be wrong. Very few people know how to listen properly, and Momo's way of listening was quite unique.[9]

Momo just sits there and listens. But her listening works wonders. She gives people ideas that would never have occurred to them on their own. Her listening is actually reminiscent of Hermann Broch's hospitable listening, which frees the Other for themselves:

> She simply sat there and listened with the utmost attention and sympathy, fixing them with her big, dark eyes, and they suddenly became aware of ideas whose existence they had never suspected.

Momo could listen in such a way that worried and indecisive people knew their own minds from one moment to the next, or shy people felt suddenly confident and at ease, or downhearted people felt happy and hopeful. And if someone felt that his life had been an utter failure, and that he himself was only one among millions of wholly unimportant people who could be replaced as easily as broken windowpanes, he would go and pour out his heart to Momo. And, even as he spoke, he would come to realize by some mysterious means that he was absolutely wrong: that there was only one person like himself in the whole world, and that, consequently, he mattered to the world in his own particular way.

Such was Momo's talent for listening.[10]

Listening gives everyone back what is *theirs*. Momo also resolves conflict merely through pure listening:

> Another time, a little boy brought her his canary because it wouldn't sing. Momo found that a far harder proposition. She had to sit and listen to the bird for a whole week before it finally started to trill and warble again.[11]

The noisy society of fatigue is deaf. The society to come, by contrast, could be termed a *society of listeners and hearkeners*. What is needed today is a *temporal revolution* that ushers in a completely different time; we must rediscover the *time of the Other*. Today's temporal crisis is not acceleration, but rather the totalization of the *time of the self*. The time of the Other eludes the logic of increase based on performance and efficiency, which creates a pressure to accelerate. The neoliberal politics of time does away with the time of the Other, which it considers an unproductive time. The totalization of the time of the self goes hand in hand with the totalization of production, which affects all areas of contemporary life and leads to the total exploitation of humans. The neoliberal politics of time also does away with the time of celebration, the time of joyful bloom, which evades the logic of production. For it is concerned with *de-production*. Unlike the time of the self, which isolates and separates us, the time of the Other creates a *community*. It is therefore a *good time*.

Notes

Chapter 1 The Terror of the Same

1 'Performance' [*Leistung*] is used here in the sense of functioning level and achievement, not performativity (transl.).

2 Han, like Heidegger in the passage quoted below, distinguishes between *das Selbe* and *das Gleiche*, both of which can be translated as 'the same'; the difference lies in the fact that the former refers to a single thing (for example, several people living in the same house) and the latter to things that are equal or equivalent, but still separate (for example, various people driving the same model of car). It would be logical to translate them as 'same' and 'equal' respectively, but because of the other connotations of the word 'equal' and the fact that Han focuses here on the contrast between *das Andere* [the Other] and *das Gleiche*, a pairing that is more logically translated as 'the Other' and 'the same', *das Selbe* has been translated here not as 'the

same', but rather 'the selfsame', even if this has a slightly different tone compared to the everyday character of the German words. For the sake of consistency, the same principle has been applied to the Heidegger quotation, where the published translation originally had 'the same' for *das Selbe* and 'the equal' for *das Gleiche* (transl.).

3 Martin Heidegger, "'...Poetically, Man Dwells...'", transl. Albert Hofstadter, in *Philosophical and Political Writings*, ed. Manfred Stassen (New York: Continuum, 2003), p. 269 (translation modified).

4 Eli Pariser, *The Filter Bubble: How the New Personalized Web Is Changing What We Read and How We Think* (New York: Penguin, 2011), p. 15.

5 Martin Heidegger, *On the Way to Language*, transl. Peter D. Hertz (New York: Harper & Row, 1971), p. 57.

6 The original word *Erkenntnis* is often translated in philosophical texts as 'knowledge', which fails to capture the active process of (re)cognition. As the contrast between the active attainment of knowledge and the passivity of mere information is central here, *Erkenntnis* has consistently been translated as 'insight' (transl.).

7 Max Scheler, 'Love and Knowledge', in *On Feeling, Knowing, and Valuing: Selected Writings*, ed. Harold J. Bershady (Chicago and London: University of Chicago Press, 1992), p. 164. The translation has been modified to reflect the concerns outlined in note 6, though the title – original *Liebe und Erkenntnis* – has been retained on account of its publication under this name.

8 Paul Celan, *Breathturn Into Timestead: The Complete Later Poetry*, transl. Pierre Joris (New York: Farrar, Straus & Giroux), pp. 87f.

9 Vilém Flusser, *Kommunikologie weiter denken: Die Bochumer Vorlesungen* (Frankfurt: Fischer, 2009), p. 251.

10 For the sake of readability and maintaining the wordplay

of the original, the word normally translated as 'same' [*gleich*] has here been rendered as 'equal', but should be taken (in this case) as synonymous (transl.).

11 Walter Benjamin, *The Arcades Project*, ed. Rolf Tiedemann, transl. Howard Eiland and Kevin McLaughlin (Cambridge, MA: Harvard University Press, 1999), p. 447.

12 Jean Baudrillard, *The Ecstasy of Communication*, ed. Sylvère Lotringer, transl. Bernard and Caroline Schutze (New York: Semiotext(e), 1988), p. 48.

13 Jean Baudrillard, *Fatal Strategies*, ed. Jim Fleming, transl. Philip Beitchmann and W. G. J. Niesluchowski (Los Angeles: Semiotext(e), 1990), p. 54.

14 Ibid., p. 51.

15 Ibid.

Chapter 2 The Violence of the Global and Terrorism

1 The author here plays on the twofold character of the word for 'compare', *vergleichen*, whose unused but literal meaning is 'equalize, make the same', by occasionally hyphenating its noun form as *Ver-Gleichen*. Although 'compare' has a similar structure, its Latinate character (Lat. *par*, 'equal') makes it difficult to introduce the manipulation of the German, which would be 'com-*pare*'. In any case, its precise etymological basis – *cum*, 'with' and *par*, 'the same' – still fails to match the German, as the prefix *ver-* usually indicates one thing acting upon and often changing another; it would thus be more consistent and logical if *vergleichen* actually meant 'equalize' rather than 'compare'. As there seems to be no satisfactory equivalent in English, the hyphenated form has simply been translated as either 'compare' or 'equalize', depending on the emphasis in the given passage (transl.).

2 Carl Schmitt, *Theory of the Partisan: Intermediate Commentary on the Concept of the Political*, transl. G. L.

Ulmen (New York: Telos, 2007), p. 85 (translation modified).

3 See note 10 (transl.).

4 'Jean Baudrillard im Gespräch mit Peter Engelmann', in Jean Baudrillard, *Der Geist des Terrorismus* (Vienna: Passagen, 2002), p. 54 (this interview does not appear in the English-language edition, *The Spirit of Terrorism*, transl. Chris Turner (London and New York: Verso, 2003)).

5 Jean Baudrillard, *The Transparency of Evil: Essays on Extreme Phenomena*, transl. James Benedict (London and New York: Verso, 1993), p. 74.

6 Baudrillard, *Der Geist des Terrorismus*, p. 54.

7 Winfried Menninghaus, *Disgust: Theory and History of a Strong Sensation*, transl. Howard Eiland and Joel Golb (Albany, NY: SUNY Press, 2003), p. 1 (translation modified).

8 See Theodor W. Adorno, *Negative Dialectics*, transl. E. B. Ashton (New York: Continuum, 1972), p. 191.

9 Immanuel Kant, 'Toward Perpetual Peace', in *Toward Perpetual Peace and Other Writings on Politics, Peace, and History*, ed. Pauline Klingfeld, transl. David L. Clocasure (New Haven: Yale University Press, 2006), p. 92.

10 Johann Wolfgang von Goethe, *Faust, Part Two*, transl. David Luke (Oxford and New York: Oxford University Press, 1994), p. 211 (l. 11186–11188).

11 Kant, 'Toward Perpetual Peace', p. 82.

12 Ibid.

13 Ibid.

14 Ibid., pp. 84f.

15 Friedrich Nietzsche, *Nachgelassene Fragmente Juli 1882– Winter 1883–1884, Kritische Gesamtausgabe* VII1 (Berlin and New York: de Gruyter, 1973), p. 240. The word for 'hospitality' is *Gastfreundschaft*, which literally means 'guest-friendship' (transl.).

16 Friedrich Nietzsche, *The Gay Science*, transl. Josefine Nauckhoff and Adrian Del Caro (Cambridge: Cambridge University Press, 2001), p. 186.

Chapter 3 *The Terror of Authenticity*

1 Roland Barthes, *A Lover's Discourse: Fragments*, transl. Richard Howard (London: Penguin, 1990), p. 35.
2 Sigmund Freud, *Introductory Lectures on Psychoanalysis*, transl. James Strachey (London: Penguin, 1990), pp. 470f.
3 Sigmund Freud, 'Beyond the Pleasure Principle', transl. James Strachey, in *The Penguin Freud Reader*, ed. Adam Phillips (London: Penguin, 2006), p. 179.
4 Karl-Heinz Bohrer, 'Authentizität und Terror', in *Nach der Natur. Über Politik und Ästhetik* (Munich and Vienna: Hanser, 1988), p. 259.

Chapter 4 *Anxiety*

1 Martin Heidegger, *Being and Time*, transl. John Macquarrie and Edward Robinson (New York: Harper & Row, 1962), pp. 233f.
2 Ibid., p. 164.
3 The choice of 'authenticity' for *Eigentlichkeit* in the 1962 translation is not unproblematic, but has established itself in the Anglophone discourse and seems no more flawed than the alternatives proposed elsewhere. Where Heideggerian 'authenticity' is meant rather than its more conventional sense, the German term has been used (transl.).
4 Ibid., p. 222.
5 Ibid., p. 249.
6 Martin Heidegger, *History of the Concept of Time: Prolegomena*, transl. Theodore Kisiel (Bloomington and Indianapolis: Indiana University Press, 2009), p. 313.

7   Heidegger, *Being and Time*, p. 369.
8   Martin Heidegger, *Contributions to Philosophy (of the Event)*, transl. Richard Rojcewicz and Daniela Vallega-Neu (Bloomington and Indianapolis: Indiana University Press, 2012), p. 224.
9   Martin Heidegger, 'The Thing', in *Poetry, Language, Thought*, transl. Albert Hofstadter (New York: Harper & Row, 1971), p. 179.
10 Georg Wilhelm Friedrich Hegel, *Phenomenology of Spirit*, transl. A. V. Miller (Oxford and New York: Oxford University Press, 1977), p. 19 (translation modified).
11 Martin Heidegger, *The Fundamental Concepts of Metaphysics: World, Finitude, Solitude*, transl. William McNeill and Nicholas Walker (Bloomington and Indianapolis: Indiana University Press, 1995), p. 131.
12 Ibid., p. 152.
13 The word for 'particular', *bestimmt*, here plays on *Stimme*, meaning 'voice' (transl.).
14 Heidegger, *Pathmarks*, p. 234.
15 Ibid., p. 233.
16 Martin Heidegger, *Parmenides*, transl. André Schuwer and Richard Rojcewicz (Bloomington and Indianapolis: Indiana University Press, 1998), p. 166.
17 Quoted in Philippe Mengue, *Faire l'idiot: La politique de Deleuze* (Paris: Germina, 2013), p. 7.
18 Heidegger, *Pathmarks*, p. 243.
19 Heinz Bude, *Gesellschaft der Angst* (Hamburg: Hamburger Edition HIS, 2014), p. 26.
20 Ibid., p. 24.

Chapter 5 Thresholds
1   Peter Handke, *Phantasien der Repetition* (Frankfurt: Suhrkamp, 1983), p. 13.
2   Baudrillard, *The Ecstasy of Communication*, p. 27.

Chapter 6 Alienation

1 British editions of Camus's novel have used the title *The Outsider*, American ones *The Stranger*. The German title is *Der Fremde* [The Stranger], which is a more accurate rendering of the original *L'Etranger* and connects it to the discussion of foreignness [*Fremdheit*] and strangers in this section (transl.).

2 Paul Celan, *Selections*, ed. and transl. Pierre Joris (Berkeley and Los Angeles: University of California Press, 2005), pp. 63f.

3 Karl Marx, *Economic and Philosophic Manuscripts of 1844*, ed. and transl. Martin Milligan (Mineola, NY: Dover, 2007), p. 69.

4 Ibid., p. 70.

Chapter 7 Counter-body

1 Martin Heidegger, 'Why Do I Stay in the Provinces?' (1934), transl. Thomas Sheehan, in *Heidegger: The Man and the Thinker*, ed. Thomas Sheehan (Chicago: Precedent, 1981), p. 27.

2 'Counterpart' is used here for *Gegenüber*, and is not especially satisfactory; the German word is a continuation of the 'against' [*gegen*] theme, which is admittedly present in 'counter', but the original refers substantially to some form of communication partner, someone or something metaphorically 'opposite' (its adjectival form is used in the straightforward sense of something being physically opposite to something else). It thus emphasizes the combination of otherness and engagement, and in a different context might well be translated as 'other', but the extensive use of that term in the present text precludes such a choice (transl.).

3 Hubert Winkels, *Leselust und Bildermacht: Literatur, Fernsehen und Neue Medien* (Frankfurt: Suhrkamp, 1999), pp. 80f.

4 Peter Handke, *A Journey to the Rivers: Justice for Serbia*, transl. Scott Abbott (New York: Viking, 1997), p. 40.

5 Martin Heidegger, *The Principle of Reason*, transl. Reginald Lilly (Bloomington and Indianapolis: Indiana University Press, 1991), p. 82.

6 Ibid.

Chapter 8 Gaze

1 Maurice Blanchot, *Thomas the Obscure*, transl. Robert Lamberton (New York: Station Hill Press, 1988), p. 25.

2 *The Ethics of Psychoanalysis 1959–1960: The Seminar of Jacques Lacan*, Book VII, ed. Jacques-Alain Miller, transl. Dennis Porter (London: Routledge, 1999), p. 253.

3 *Anxiety: The Seminar of Jacques Lacan*, Book X, ed. Jacques-Alain Miller, transl. A. R. Price (Cambridge: Polity, 2014), p. 254.

4 See *Everything You Always Wanted to Know about Lacan (But Were Afraid to Ask Hitchcock)*, ed. Slavoj Žižek (London and New York: Verso, 1992).

5 Jean-Paul Sartre, *Being and Nothingness: An Essay on Phenomenological Ontology*, transl. Hazel E. Barnes (New York: Washington Square Press, 1992), p. 346. Barnes's translation uses 'look' rather than 'gaze' (transl.).

6 Michel Foucault, *Discipline and Punish: The Birth of the Prison*, transl. Alan Sheridan (New York: Vintage, 1977), p. 195.

7 George Orwell, *Nineteen Eighty-Four* (London: Penguin, 1987), p. 3.

Chapter 9 Voice

1 Franz Kafka, *The Castle: A New Translation Based on the Restored Text* (New York: Schocken, 1998), p. 20.

2 Ibid., p. 36.

3 Ibid.
4 Franz Kafka, 'Investigations of a Dog', in *A Hunger Artist and Other Stories*, transl. Joyce Crick (Oxford and New York: Oxford University Press, 2012), p. 150.
5 Ibid.
6 Franz Kafka, *Letters to Milena*, transl. Philip Boehm (New York: Schocken, 1990), p. 30.
7 Roland Barthes, 'The Grain of the Voice', in *Image Music Text*, ed. and transl. Stephen Heath (London: Fontana, 1977), p. 188.
8 Kafka, *Letters to Milena*, p. 223.
9 Barthes, 'The Grain of the Voice', pp. 181f.
10 Ibid., p. 182.
11 Ibid., p. 183.
12 Ibid., p. 184.
13 Ibid.
14 Ibid.
15 Novalis, *Briefe und Werke*, ed. P. Kluckhohn (Berlin: Kohlhammer, 1943), vol. 3, no. 1140.
16 Daniel Paul Schreber, *Memoirs of My Nervous Illness*, ed. and transl. Ida Macalpine and Richard A. Hunter (London: W. Dawson, 1955) , p. 35.
17 Ibid., p. 249.
18 Ibid., p. 123n.
19 Immanuel Kant, *Critique of Practical Reason*, revised edn, ed. and transl. Mary Gregor (Cambridge: Cambridge University Press, 2015), p. 66.
20 Heidegger, *Being and Time*, p. 313.
21 Ibid., p. 206.
22 Ibid.
23 Heidegger, *The Principle of Reason*, p. 50.
24 Martin Heidegger, *Elucidations of Hölderlin's Poetry*, transl. Keith Hoeller (New York: Humanity Books, 2000) p. 193.
25 *'Mein liebes Seelchen!' Briefe Martin Heideggers an seine*

Frau Elfride 1915–1970, ed. Gertrud Heidegger (Munich: Deutsche Verlags-Anstalt, 2005), p. 264.

26 Paul Celan, *The Meridian: Final Version-Drafts-Materials*, ed. Bernhard Böschenstein and Heine Schmull, transl. Pierre Joris (Stanford University Press, 2011), p. 11.

Chapter 10 The Language of the Other

1 Theodor W. Adorno, *Aesthetic Theory*, transl. Robert Hullot-Kentor (London and New York: Bloomsbury, 2013), p. 173.

2 The word rendered here as 'disconcerting' is *befremdend* (based on *fremd*, 'strange/foreign'; see note 1 of ch, 6), which could be more literally translated as 'estranging'.

3 Adorno, *Aesthetic Theory*, p. 173 (translation modified).

4 See Theodor W. Adorno, *Minima Moralia: Reflections from a Damaged Life*, transl. Edmund N. Jephcott (London and New York: Verso, 2005), pp. 89f.

5 Celan, *The Meridian*, p. 5.

6 Heidegger, *Poetry, Language, Thought*, p. 226 (translation modified).

7 Celan, *The Meridian*, p. 7.

8 Peter Handke, *Die Geschichte des Bleistifts* (Frankfurt: Suhrkamp, 1985), p. 353.

9 Ibid., p. 346.

10 Celan, *The Meridian*, p. 6.

11 Ibid.

12 Handke, *Die Geschichte des Bleistifts*, p. 352.

13 Interview for *DIE ZEIT*, 12 July 2012.

14 Celan, *The Meridian*, p. 8.

15 Ibid., p. 9 (translation modified).

16 Ibid.

17 Emmanuel Levinas, *Totality and Infinity: An Essay on Exteriority*, transl. Alphonso Lingis (Dordrecht: Kluwer Academic Publishers, 2012), p. 178.

18 Celan, *The Meridian*, p. 9.
19 Ibid.
20 Ibid.
21 See Martin Buber, 'Distance and Relation', transl. by Ronald Gregor Smith, *The Hibbert Journal*, vol. XLIX (January 1951).
22 Martin Buber, *I and Thou*, transl. Walter Kaufmann (New York: Touchstone, 1996), p. 84.

Chapter 11 The Thinking of the Other

1 Emmanuel Levinas, *Time and the Other*, transl. Richard A. Cohen (Pittsburgh: Duquesne University Press, 1987), p. 56.
2 Emmanuel Levinas, *Existence and Existents*, transl. Alphonso Lingis (Dordrecht: Kluwer Academic Publishers, 1988), p. 30.
3 Levinas, *Time and the Other*, p. 72.
4 Ibid., p. 88.
5 Emmanuel Levinas, *Otherwise Than Being, or Beyond Essence*, transl. Alphonso Lingis (Dordrecht: Kluwer Academic Publishers, 1991), p. 51.
6 Ibid., p. 77.
7 Emmanuel Levinas, *Discovering Existence with Husserl*, transl. Richard A. Cohen (Evanston: Northwestern University Press, 1998), p. 111.
8 Friedrich Nietzsche, *Human, All Too Human: A Book for Free Spirits*, transl. R. J. Hollingdale (Cambridge: Cambridge University Press, 1996), pp. 229f.
9 Alain Badiou, 'What Is Love?', trans. Justin Clemens, in *Sexuation: SIC 3*, ed. Renata Salecl (Durham and London: Duke University Press, 2000), p. 270. 'Stage' is meant here in the theatrical sense (transl.).
10 Levinas, *Otherwise Than Being*, p. 6.

Chapter 12 Listening

1 Elias Canetti, *The Play of the Eyes*, transl. Ralph Manheim (London: Granta, 1986), p. 29.
2 Ibid., p. 30.
3 Ibid.
4 Ibid., p. 25.
5 Elias Canetti, *The Human Province*, transl. Joachim Neugroschel (New York: Seabury Press, 1978), p. 243.
6 Elias Canetti, *The Agony of Flies: Notes and Notations*, transl. H. F. Broch de Rothermann (New York: Farrar, Straus & Giroux, 1994).
7 Canetti, *The Human Province*, p. 248.
8 Michael Ende, *Momo*, transl. J. Maxwell Brownjohn (London: Puffin, 1985), p. 19.
9 Ibid., p. 18.
10 Ibid., pp. 18f.
11 Ibid., p. 23.